Awakening Your Business Brain

"In today's media-rich landscape, the music industry has changed dramatically and is rapidly shifting on a daily basis. In this environment, musicians and executives alike must think creatively and be entrepreneurial. iCadenza's *Awakening Your Business Brain* provides an excellent foundation for developing the kind of mindset that will provide musicians with the critical competitive advantage necessary to survive—and thrive—in the ever-evolving business of music. Having been on just about every side of this industry—as a musician, producer, and film music executive—I remember learning many of these lessons along the way. Reading this book will likely save musicians time and help them find success faster."
- Paul Broucek, President, Warner Bros. Pictures - Music

"*Awakening Your Business Brain* is an excellent book that helps musicians break through obstacles and take action towards their career goals. It is especially helpful for key areas that pose a challenge to many musicians, including self-promotion, negotiation and networking. Julia and Jennifer have written a valuable book that can benefit all musicians, regardless of career stage."
- Aaron P. Dworkin, Dean, University of Michigan School of Music, Theatre & Dance; Member, The National Council on the Arts; Founder, Sphinx Organization

"If the words 'business' or 'marketing' make you feel icky and uncomfortable, this book will open your eyes to a different path, as Julia and Jennifer gently debunk prevalent myths about business, and reveal how making a good living in music is as much a mindset as it is a function of talent, hard work, creativity, and skill."
- Noa Kageyama, M.M., Ph.D., Performance Psychologist, Faculty, The Juilliard School, *www.bulletproofmusician.com*

"This book is thoughtfully and expertly put together and I think will help a great many artists on their journey. I admire very much the careful and caring way [Jennifer and Julia] have put it together."
- Frederica von Stade, Mezzo-Soprano

"I wish such a book had existed when I was starting out in my career. I feel I have learned lots of these principles along the way but having had them at the beginning would have been amazing. I will recommend this book to many of my students and, perhaps, use it in a course at my university which will be a great tool to musicians embarking on their careers. Bravi, Julia and Jennifer!"
- Elizabeth Futral, Coloratura Soprano

"There is infinite opportunity in the modern musical world and this publication from iCadenza will help any aspiring musician find their place in it. The book offers advice that will empower musicians to find happiness and defines success in a way that can feel attainable to an artist at any stage of their career!"
- Michael Alexander, Director, School of Music, University of Northern Colorado

"*Awakening your Business Brain: An iCadenza Guide to Launching your Music Career* awakens us all, emerging artists and longtime academics alike, to trust in a thriving career, but only when assumptions welcome questioning, optimism accompanies feasibility, and creativity is unleashed through the art as well as the art of composing your own best career.

"This practical, positive, and proactive how-to guide is appropriately authored by the dynamic-duo of music entrepreneurship. Jennifer Rosenfeld is smarter than any two Deans I have met combined, and Julia Torgovitskaya couples the artistry earned on stage with an unfaltering passion for nurturing musicians to take charge of their own most promising futures."
- Dr. Mark Rabideau, Director, 21st-Century Musician Initiative, DePauw University

"*Awakening Your Business Brain* is a brilliant, remarkably practical guide that will help you...there's no other way to put it...turn your dreams of a life in music into reality. The authors are insightful, sensitive, engaging, and always connected to the real and psychological obstacles that face sensitive artists trying to make a career. I can't think of a better book on this subject."
- Gail Eichenthal, Executive Producer of KUSC and KDFC

"Julia and Jennifer have been working with aspiring musicians for over 6 years to help them "awaken their business brain." They have taken their successful case study experiences and distilled them into an easy to read, easy to learn, easy to implement e-book."
- John Rehfeld, former CEO of Proxima, Toshiba computer division and Seiko USA, currently CEO/business coach, professor of marketing/strategy at Pepperdine and USD

Awakening your Business Brain

An iCadenza Guide to Launching your Music Career

You are enjoying an iCadenza book!

To learn more about iCadenza and what
Jennifer and Julia can do for your
music career, visit:

http://www.icadenza.com/

Thanks for reading!

Table of Contents

Acknowledgements

Writing a book has been a dream of ours for several years and we are indebted to so many people who helped make this dream a reality. First and foremost, we are so grateful to Adrianne Munkacsy and Hannah Sternberg, our book team, who worked tirelessly to polish and launch this project.

Thank you to our clients and colleagues who provided so many of the learning moments that inspired this book. You'll get to meet a number of them in the pages that follow, though they may appear sometimes with altered names to protect their privacy. And a major thank you to the Cadenza Artists team for your support and encouragement – and for keeping the ship afloat when we did our writing retreat, especially Greg Kastelman, Ben Cohen, Anjin Stewart-Funai, Cheri Jamison, Maria Elena O'Connor, and Cindy Hwang.

And, most of all, thank you to our families for your never-ending support, and invaluable feedback on this book.

Introduction

You've sacrificed in the name of art. You've spent years conquering music theory and history classes. You've braved the classroom and performance hall to reach that coveted music degree. And, of course, you've practiced, practiced, practiced (after all, that's the only way to Carnegie Hall, right?).

So here you are. Ready to unleash your talent onto the world. There's just one problem: you have no idea what the next steps are.

The only paths available to you are flooded by an endless sea of other musicians. Everyone talks about networking, but you don't know anyone who can help you get your foot in the door; you only know other musicians just like you.

People tell you to get your business chops together, but that sounds like the opposite of being an artist (and it also sounds a little scary). You worry that tapping into your business brain means you're selling out.

You don't know how you're ever going to balance your high level of artistry with the "administrative" work required to get your name out there.

You're in the Right Place

The good news is that you're not alone. And while the artistry and the passion that you bring to the world are unique (we're going to help you double down on your uniqueness factor), your challenges are not.

We wrote this book for two main reasons.

The first is to debunk some of the limiting and inaccurate judgments that many artists hold about business. Some of these are ideas that are formed very early in an artist's training, long before our professional years. It's time to let these ideas go.

The second reason is to give you practical tools for creating a music career that you love.

That's why we want to make a deal with you. Based on our work helping artists barrel through challenges similar to what you're facing, we're certain that, if you take our words seriously, you'll see traction in your life and career within a year.

Your end of the bargain is to temporarily suspend your disbelief, judgment, and doubts, and follow the processes that we outline in the pages to come. Try out the exercises. Play around with shifting your mindset. Give this new way a fair shot.

How We Got Here

We've been through dark moments just like you.

Today, we're lucky to do what we love and to live our lives out loud with passion. But we struggled to get here.

Having grown up in families that instilled a love for music into our bones, our childhoods were infused with music-making. In fact, we met back when we were thirteen or fourteen in choir at our middle school.

We were inspired to fall in love with music by the music director at our high school, Timothy Bruneau. A man who never passed up an opportunity to turn an awkward moment into a lifelong lesson through music, his love of music and art was contagious. He challenged us to view music as a powerful vehicle of both expression and connection. He also pushed us to the brink of what we thought was possible, inspiring us to start our quest for mastery—because he believed in our ability to reach it. We were hooked.

We also had some of our most important learning experiences when creating music together. We witnessed each other's most painful growing moments during the "awkward" teen years, and we got through them together.

Although we wound up on opposite coasts in college (Julia went to Tufts, Jennifer to Stanford), we remained friends. For many years, we continued to immerse ourselves in music. We studied theory, tried our hands at composition, performed as much as we could, and, of course, practiced, practiced, practiced.

We had amazing triumphs and suffered painful defeats. We experienced firsthand the hamster wheel of pursuing a career as a musician.

During our senior years, we talked seriously about starting a business in the performing arts industry. We saw a lot of challenges in that field— a field we'd been enamored with for most of our lives—and we were just naïve and presumptuous enough to think that we could singlehandedly change them. We didn't know then what we know now. We've had to learn it along the way. Luckily, we didn't know how hard it would be, so we didn't succumb to the fear and resistance that surely would have stopped us in our tracks if we'd known better. Now we know how to pull ourselves together when we go through fear and uncertainty (and we'll share some of that with you in the pages that follow), but at that time, we didn't know about that stuff yet.

On a lark, we entered the Social Entrepreneurship division of Tufts University's Gordon Institute Business Plan Competition, highlighted by *Forbes* as one of the fifteen biggest university-sponsored competitions. We won second place, and we haven't looked back.

Over the years, we've come to believe wholeheartedly that business is fundamentally a creative and inspiring endeavor, and that it requires as much vision and gumption as honing one's artistic craft.

We now run two companies, and have worked with over a thousand artists through consulting, artist management, talent representation, online courses, workshops, and retreats. We've also interviewed more than 200 musicians, from emerging artists to the most successful A-listers like Hilary Hahn and Marilyn Horne.

Through our consulting company, iCadenza, we work with musicians and performing artists to help them discover their voices as creators, forge their paths, build their networks, and develop a following.

We've helped artists launch new organizations and groups, secure donors and funding, book gigs and arrange tours, launch authentic and impactful promotional strategies, and win major positions at organizations and institutions.

Our proudest moments, however, are when we have the privilege of supporting clients in renewing their sense of self, recommitting to their passion, knocking down fears and concerns, and stepping into their power as savvy, business-minded professionals.

Our consulting work led to the formation of our talent agency and artist management company, Cadenza Artists. In the short time since its launch, Cadenza Artists has attracted some of the most talented, visionary artists appearing on today's stages, ranging from two-time Grammy Award winning violinist Mark O'Connor to contemporary performance projects like DJ Kid Koala's *Nufonia Must Fall.*

By cultivating a staff of extraordinarily creative, client-focused agents and arts professionals who are deeply passionate about the performing arts, Cadenza Artists has experienced rapid growth in both U.S. and international markets, and is quickly evolving into a recognized and respected artist management company and talent agency.

Through our work, we've seen a lot of what happens on both sides of the fence – the artist side and the venue/presenter side. So much of our work with iCadenza has focused on supporting artists during that in-between stage after completing one's education and before "making it" – whether that means securing a manager, having an active touring career, or another definition of success.

This book is similarly geared towards creative individuals in that in-between state, as well as students and professionals who have "made it" but are still striving for a higher level of fulfillment. The strategies we share are both those that we've used to grow our own business, and the ones we've seen work best for our clients.

How to Use This Book

We recommend you read this book in order the first time through because each chapter builds upon the one before it. After going through it once, you can return to the chapters or practice exercises that are best suited for where you are in your career right now.

Speaking of practice exercises, each chapter has a "Putting It into Practice" section. We encourage you to have a journal handy and commit to spending time working on the questions and activities we propose. You might be surprised at the insights you'll gain if you spend just ten or fifteen minutes reflecting.

Your Mindset Matters

Through our intensive client work, (and, frankly, through our own work), we've observed common thought patterns, mindsets and behaviors that work for people—and those that don't. In our experience, we have found that the most powerful tools in our arsenal are always our ability to understand, deeply support, and work on our own selves and our own mindset.

We wrote this book to help you let go of the things that don't work and hold fast to those that do. Our goal is to help you achieve your big vision faster and with less stress.

We won't be sharing with you any gimmicks or shortcuts. Why? Because they don't exist. Instead, we're going to help you face the realities of the music business today, and give you real, ready-to-apply tips to address each and every one of the most common problems that the artists we've encountered tend to experience. We'll be sharing lots of personal examples as well as some that we're "borrowing" from friends and clients of ours, to show—not tell—what we're hoping to get across to you. And we'll help you succeed in a way that facilitates greater authenticity and fulfillment.

Are you ready?

Chapter 1
Assumptions About Business: Real or Imagined?

Business. Entrepreneurship. Sales. With social media and technology turning everyone into a potential small business owner, these buzzwords have become ever-present in our lives.

Now, they're invading music and the arts! Musicians are expected to be effective business people, capable of "selling themselves," being entrepreneurs, and understanding all the administrative and marketing tasks that go along with that.

As a musician, you've had to work for years, if not decades, on honing your craft. It's a little painful to think about all those hours spent in the practice room, all the corrections from (usually) well-meaning teachers, all the lost sleep, all those party invitations that you had to pass on...so much sacrifice in service of creating something extraordinary onstage, something so technically perfect and artistically astute that the impact on a listener might be life-changing.

And now the experts are throwing this "business" business in your face like it's something you're just supposed to pick up!

It's enough to make you throw your hands up and lose faith in your dream.

But that's only if you look at the business of music as something negative. We'll get more into what the business of music means to us in chapter 3. But first, let's tackle some of the common assumptions that musicians make about business that cast it in a negative light. We aren't bringing up these assumptions to dwell on the negative. Instead, our hope is to put them out on the table so that we can have a full picture of the mental landscape in which we musicians are inclined to reside. We'll debunk these assumptions throughout the rest of this book (and specifically in the next two chapters) to help you more positively relate to the business of the arts. We will show you how (at least on a good day) we manage to turn our own would-be stress or anxiety triggers into fun and empowering triggers, instead. If you follow our lead, we promise you that over the course of these chapters you'll see how business can be creative, inspiring, and even fun! And if you're like us, you'll be surprised to see how adaptable we humans can be. Are you ready?

Assumption #1: Business Is Only About Sales and That's Not How I Relate to Art.

Many artists feel that business is inherently soulless and purely about sales, bottom lines, and money.

If business is all about money, then that is certainly not how an artist wishes to define herself. Art can be deeply meaningful on the most personal level, not only to its creator, but to its audience as well. How can something so deep and meaningful be reduced to dollars and cents?

While money *does* matter (it's how you fund your dream, support your family, and live the lifestyle you long for), it's not all that business is about. As you'll learn throughout this book, business is about more than just the "transaction." It's about helping other people get what they want while you do what you love – an opportunity to exchange value. It's also a mindset. And once you awaken your business mindset, your music career will open up. In the chapters that follow, we'll show you how you can actually maximize your creative control through new approaches.

Assumption #2: Business Is *Not* Creative.

Often, business gets a bad reputation because the creative aspects of business may be hidden from view. We don't know much about the very secretive process of building the Apple Watch, which took over three years to develop. But there's no doubt that the process was very creative.

Developing a concept for an entirely new "product," whether it be an album, a tour, or a production, requires considerable ingenuity. Taking a business-minded approach to your project doesn't mean pandering to financial concerns. It does, however, ensure that the product that you're creating is something that people will a) want and b) know about so that they can get it. Caring about those things is not at all at odds with creativity.

Assumption #3: The Best Use of My Time Is Practicing.

Many musicians believe their only purpose is to be the best musician that they can be, delivering their most spectacular performance ever, every time they perform. To do this takes practice, so they assume that there's no time to hone their skills and focus on business at the same time.

Here's the problem with this belief: If you're practicing all the time, how will people know what you're up to? How will they get to know your work? To get noticed requires that you get out there and be seen—not just on stage during a performance, but at networking events, on social media, and in your community. *just practicing / being really good isn't enough*

Assumption #4: Business Is Boring.

Many artists assume that "business-y" stuff is boring. The notion of writing a dry, colorless business plan is only slightly less painful than a wisdom tooth extraction. As an artist, you want to grow, develop, and be open to change—and that can seem antithetical to the rigidity of business planning.

The truth is that creating a business plan can be an exciting activity! It's your opportunity to bring something new into the world. It's your chance to take an idea and turn it into an actionable plan.

As for growth and development, that's important for businesses as well. In fact, if your business is not growing, changing, and redefining itself over time, then your business won't last long.

In the lifecycle of any business, it's generally understood that a business is either growing or dying. Growth can mean growing your team, growing your sales, or allowing your project to evolve over time. Far from being boring, when your music "business" is growing you feel swept up in the momentum and freedom that it provides.

Assumption #5: Someone Else Can Do It Better than I Can.

Back when we were getting started, we assumed that seasoned entrepreneurs had their act fully together and knew what they were doing. They seemed so much smarter, sharper, faster, and more experienced than we were.

However, as we ramped up our own work in business, we learned the secret: most people have no idea what they're doing most of the time. On the one hand, that sounds like a crazy notion; how can seasoned entrepreneurs and businesspeople not know what they're doing?

On the other hand, it makes a lot of sense: musicians and entrepreneurs are building something new, something that doesn't exist yet. They can pretend to themselves and to others that they know what they're doing, but at best, they're making educated guesses and then going through a lot of trial and error to get where they need to go.

The truth is that nobody who is in the process of creating is ever certain how events will unfold. While someone else could maybe (but probably not) do a better job than you, no one will care about your project(s) as much as you do—and that counts for everything.

Assumption #6: What I Really Need Is a Manager/Agent.

"Once I'm successful, someone else will be doing this for me anyway," you might say. Let's unpack this one a bit. Sure, we all have different strengths and some people are just better with numbers, planning, details, etc. But we're not talking about buying groceries or doing your annual accounting here. We're talking about your career, your life's work.

Do you really want to put that into someone else's hands, and under someone else's control? You have this incredible opportunity to learn the ins and outs of the business that is your artistic product. Later you can hire people to help, but the only way you can be sure that you'll like the direction your career takes is if you are the captain of the ship. And, let's face it, as an artist, your career is basically your life. Do you really want to hand those reins over to someone else?

Not long ago, we had the privilege of meeting with David Foster, whose songs and guidance shaped the careers of countless pop stars, including Celine Dion, Whitney Houston, Josh Groban, Michael Bublé, and many more. He told us that the most successful pop artists are the hardest working people he knows. The press likes to highlight their partying and promiscuity, but most of the time, they're working doggedly on both their artistic output *and* the business side of their careers.

Assumption #7: My Art Speaks for Itself. I Don't Need Business to Move It Along.

Many musicians feel frustrated about having to promote themselves and their work. After all, the whole point of being a musician is communicating through music, not words! Our challenge to you is this: if you don't speak for your art, who will?

We are fortunate to live in a time when talent and amazing artistry are plentiful. The downside is that there is a lot of competition. Particularly for classical soloists doing traditional repertoire, it can be hard to tell what makes a performer unique. This is where the "speaking" part comes in. People's experience of your music is greatly enhanced if they have a positive experience of you and your brand. To get some perspective, think about it this way: in the business world, companies spend 50% of their resources on marketing and 50% on product development. Why? Because without marketing, nobody will know who they are and what they do. The same is true for you.

Assumption #8: A Product Is Not Ready to Be Sold or Presented Until It's Perfect.

Many musicians apply their extremely high artistic standards to their business process. This means that the product (promotional content, pitch, etc.) is not ready until it is perfect.

The challenge is that time goes by and "perfect" tends to linger out in the distance. How many opportunities do you miss out on while you're waiting for perfection?

And Many More Assumptions...

There may be many more thoughts and feelings that spring to mind as you consider what it means to run your artistic career as a business. Time and time again, we encounter artists who feel confused, frustrated, exasperated, and overwhelmed when they are advised to be more business-minded.

We are here to tell you that the fears and beliefs that may come up for you are totally normal. More than that, business-mindedness is a skillset that requires development and practice, just like every musical and technical skill you've built in the practice room and on stage.

The good news is that for you, someone who has worked tirelessly at honing your craft, we promise that the business side will be a lot easier to learn by comparison. And it all begins in your mind, with the willingness to let go of any unfounded assumptions you might be holding about what business is. Let's wipe the slate clean.

The Changing World

The discomfort many artists feel when challenged with creating a career they love is especially pronounced today because the music and performing arts industries have changed dramatically in the last decade, and more change is on the way.

Technology and the internet have fundamentally disrupted music business models and changed the way careers are made. Managers, record labels, and agents have less power than they once did due to these advances. On the positive side, it means that musicians who can harness these tools can shape their own destinies.

The challenge is that there is far more competition than ever before. Talent is in no short supply, and although artistry and quality matter, they aren't enough to catch a big break. Managers rarely take on a hidden gem talent with no track record; instead, they look to attach themselves to artists who are on the rise due to their own efforts.

The changes in the artist-discovery process are not the only changes that make the current landscape more difficult and competitive. Classically-trained musicians—instrumentalists, vocalists, composers, conductors—face particularly challenging landscapes due to the insolvency and disappearance of orchestras and opera companies, both great and small. When struggling companies have the funds to hire soloists for leading roles, they opt for the biggest names they can get, to attract bigger audiences. The current financial climate has made orchestra and opera managers less inclined to take a risk on emerging, lesser-known artists.

There are fewer jobs for orchestra players than ever before, and many concert seasons are shrinking. Orchestras face countless challenges—the decline of their subscriber base, many more entertainment options competing for the attention of their audiences, and a high cost structure that relies on the goodwill and solvency of donors.

As you've no doubt realized, there is a lot to be concerned about when it comes to pursuing a career in the performing arts, especially classical music. However, with every challenge comes new opportunity.

In the following chapters we will share our formula for developing the inner strengths and essential skills that you will need to survive and thrive in the career of your dreams.

To access our list of Affirmations that Banish Assumptions, and other free extras, be sure to check out **http://www.icadenza.com/ebook-resources/**

Chapter 2
Unlocking Your Assumptions

"You should only pursue a career in music if you can't do anything else."

A beloved music teacher said this to us once, and we've never forgotten it. You may have heard it too.

Without any doubt, a career in music is extremely challenging. If you can be fulfilled pursuing something else, you'll probably have an easier life.

Considering the great risks—especially financial, to say nothing of the emotional toll from the inevitable highs and lows, the quest for coveted gigs, rejections, critical reviews, and little or irregular pay—the rational person should spare him- or herself and find an easier career.

However, if you're reading this book, you've most likely taken the plunge and committed yourself to the life of a performing artist. There are two sides to this coin: the first is challenge and uncertainty. The second is the potential for unbounded fulfillment that comes with following your heart's desire.

"You should only pursue a career in music if you can't do anything else."

As we've reflected upon this statement over the years, we've realized that many musicians read into it an even darker interpretation: "If I'm pursuing a career in music, it means I can't do anything else. I lack the ability to be competent in areas other than music."

This belief reinforces the stereotype of the creative genius who lacks the basic skills of life—someone whose head is in the clouds and whose life, workspace, and taxes are in complete disarray, but who comes down to earth to deliver moments of true artistry and brilliance.

This belief also implies several assumptions about what musicians are capable of being and doing. Let's look at three primary assumptions that prevent musicians from activating their "business brain" and how to overcome them:

Assumption #1: My Brain Just Doesn't Work That Way.

Many musicians believe that being business-minded means being good at analytical, seemingly non-creative tasks like managing finances.

Musicians often claim to be bad with money. Clients have told us that their eyes glaze over when they need to prepare a budget. They sometimes realize, only after the fact, that the fees they accepted or rates they charged don't make financial sense in the bigger picture.

The Truth

Some musicians confuse business-mindedness with financial expertise and go forth convinced that they are inadequate when it comes to either. While financial mastery is a valuable skill, it's only one small part of the puzzle. Plus, it's not that different from the part of the brain that a creative person has honed so well: attention to detail.

A musician does not need to be a financial expert. He or she merely needs to be financially savvy. So, forget about fancy charts and spreadsheets. Being financially savvy is about gaining clarity concerning the money that's coming in (and when) and the money that's going out (and when). It also requires understanding your needs and wants—how much money do you need to support your desired lifestyle and the people who depend on you financially?

If you think business means turning on the financial engine, you're correct. But, that is not the whole picture. Another crucial part of your business brain is looking at the big picture of where you want to go and who you will serve along the way.

This is highly creative work, best performed by independent thinkers who can listen to their intuition and dream big. If you are passionate about saying something meaningful through your music, there is a good chance you can turn that power towards your career process.

Assumption #2: I Have to Be Starving to Be a True Artist.

The stereotype of the starving artist is alive and well, often promoted by artists themselves, even if they acknowledge the fallacy in this statement. It's not uncommon for musicians to feel uncomfortable around money and the ways to acquire it.

Many artists operate under the assumption that money is hard to come by, that no one can pay well, and that they must work tirelessly to earn a modest living for themselves and their families. They wonder: if something comes easily or pays well, is it the real deal? Or is something fishy? Is it the sign of selling out?

Musical culture has promoted a myth that if you focus on monetizing your craft you inevitably have to compromise the artistic standards you've worked tirelessly to develop. Perhaps you tell yourself, "If I'm focused on making money, I'm not focused on making art."

There is a deeper assumption here: that striving for money is selfish, even if it's to meet your basic needs or to support your family; whereas art is pure and an act of service.

If that's the case, couldn't pursuing music or art also be deemed "selfish" by that same logic? After all, it's a choice you make that honors your desires and wishes (unless, of course, you're pursuing art to please someone else, which carries its own complications).

The Truth

There's nothing wrong with following your heart's desire because you want to. It's also not wrong to want a certain lifestyle for yourself and your loved ones. Nor is it wrong to desire a level of financial stability that enables you to pick your artistic projects and to choose how you spend your time.

Beyond Finances

Often, the starving artist mentality is not just about lack of money. It can be connected to an attitude of scarcity in other areas of the artist's life, such as time. We work with clients who are stretched thin between side jobs and artistic projects that pay little to nothing. The unfortunate result is that they barely have time to devote to their art. They feel exhausted and completely spent—starved for time and creative energy. And yet they're convinced that this condition is part and parcel of being a "true" artist.

Assumption #3: I Don't Want to Be "That Guy."

You probably know someone who thinks they're rocking this social media thing by posting all over the place about how great they are doing. But maybe it's over the top and a little off-putting.

In our experience, there are just as many, if not more, humble artists who would rather not toot their own horn. However, the ones who make all the noise tend to have a bigger presence.

We talk to many artists who understand that they need to promote themselves, not just online, but offline as well. They know they need to build contacts and relationships, as well as seek partners, collaborators, and supporters, but they don't want to be "that guy."

You might be in this camp. Self-promoting, if that means acting in a way that feels arrogant and pushy, might feel totally foreign to your DNA.

The problem is that a common reaction to seeing an unsavory version of self-promotion is to do the most extreme opposite—not promoting yourself at all. Many musicians carry a belief that there's no middle ground, that self-promotion can only come across one way—and not a good way.

The Truth

With every artist we've worked with, we've found that there is another way to approach self-promotion that is both effective and feels good. The key is to tap into your authenticity. The qualities that make you special as a musician are unique to your personality, interests, passions, and history. By tapping into your authentic voice and speaking from a place of passion, you can discover a vast array of promotional opportunities that don't violate your principles.

Why You Need to Discover the Assumptions That Are Holding You Back

When we coach clients privately, we help them identify the assumptions that may be blocking their career path. Once the client has recognized the assumption as an obstacle to success, we help him or her to find a way to remove it.

Assumptions can be so deeply rooted that we might not even realize they are there. But the power of discovering, questioning, and unlocking limiting assumptions is that it makes us free. It gives us the power and freedom to take action in ways that previously were off limits. Doors that were closed or non-existent suddenly appear and open. Unlocking limiting assumptions opens up a new world of possibility--one that existed all along, but was hidden from view.

The assumptions described above are just a few examples of the thought patterns we encounter frequently. If any of these resonate for you, fear not! This book will help you shift your mindset so that you can expand your artistry and career potential in ways that never seemed possible before, through the process of awakening your business brain.

To access our list of Affirmations that Banish Assumptions, and other free extras, be sure to check out **http://www.icadenza.com/ebook-resources/**

Chapter 3
The Building Blocks of Your Business Brain

Over the next several chapters we will discuss the six pillars of action and behavior that will make you unstoppable.

You might be surprised to find that they won't seem very "business-y." There won't be any buzzwords or cheap sales tactics, and minimal conversation about finances. That's because, in our view, the business brain, more than anything else, is a way of looking at the world that motivates and guides you toward meaningful action.

Before we get into the substance, we will set the stage with a few basic principles to keep in mind as you continue reading. We'll also share our definition of business and what it means to us. Lastly, we will discuss some of our experiences developing our clients' business brains, and our own as well.

In order to succeed today, musicians need to adopt attitudes that might feel unfamiliar, but will soon become second nature once the tangible benefits emerge. At the core, we believe that success results from two basic behaviors:

1. **Openness to growth and learning:** Are you willing to let go of how you see the world and experiment with a new mindset? Are you willing to be a beginner and pick up new

skills that might feel foreign and uncomfortable?

2. **A bias toward action:** Are you willing to take consistent action on a regular basis to move toward your goals? By action, we mean engaging in the key activities that are most crucial to achieving your short- and long-term objectives, even if you work in tiny, baby-step increments.

With these behaviors in hand, the most successful artists possess a clear vision for what they want to offer and an optimistic outlook about their ability to achieve it. Successful artists know what is uniquely theirs to offer and believe in their ability to deliver a quality product to a target audience.

But, let's consider the reverse. If you, as an artist, doubt your uniqueness, how can you identify the niche or niches to which your artistry belongs? How can you even define your target audience? If this is your predicament, let us examine how you might have gotten there.

During years of musical training, is it possible that you adopted attitudes and habits that have clouded your judgment about your artistry, and hindered your efforts to turn your uniqueness into a success story?

Consider whether some of the admirable and essential qualities ingrained in you through years of musical training might be standing in the way of your career progress, such as:

- keen, unwavering focus on details
- a sharp, critical ear
- striving toward perfection (nothing is ready to be seen until it is perfect)

- repetition of the same tasks over and over again. While the repertoire changes, the process often stays the same and becomes an area of strong competency.

These all sound positive, right?

They're all crucial skills, both for music and life, but they can come into conflict with the qualities that are required for career growth. Consider the following:

- Can you let go of the details for a moment and step back and think about the big picture?
- Can you let go of self-judgment? When we judge ourselves harshly, we tend to judge others as well. Also, we can fall into the pattern of assuming that others will be as judgmental towards us as we are to ourselves.
- Can you experiment with letting go of perfectionism and adopt a willingness to put yourself out there, even if you're not "fully cooked?"
- Can you get comfortable with being uncomfortable and accept a beginner's mindset for the skills and behaviors that feel foreign and unnatural?

With this new framing in mind, let's dig into what business is when it comes to your life and career. We bet you that our definition of business will feel much more authentic to the artistic, creative types out there. Even more importantly, it will help you to become much more effective in growing your career and managing the "business" aspects of what you do.

What *Is* Business?

At its core, business is the method by which you exchange value with others and grow the opportunities to exchange that value. The underlying principle is that you have something important and valuable to offer, something that will change people's lives by giving them an experience that enables them to view the world in a new way, even if only for the duration of your performance.

As we will discuss in chapter 4, connecting to your value and why it matters is key. Once you recognize how valuable your music, performance, and skills are, your job is to enable the right people to experience that value.

It might take some work to figure out who those people are, how to find them, and how to speak to them. You'll need to develop a fined-tuned understanding of what they want and need. Once you do that, you create opportunities and touchpoints to exchange your value for something in return (usually money).

Of course, we can receive value back in a multitude of ways. But, let's not forget why you are here: you desire to expand your career as a musician—which means you want to receive financial compensation for the various music-related services and products you provide.

Know Who You're in Business For

The concept of compensation in exchange for value leads to a very important topic. If you want to make a living as a musician, you need awareness of your target audience.

Many musicians have a unique artistic vision that is grounded in the philosophy of "I make music that *I* like. I play for myself, not for anyone else." There's nothing wrong with this attitude as far as music-making is concerned. You are most proud of your work when you feel that it represents you honestly.

But, if you have no regard for what your audience wants or thinks, you'll have a hard time turning music into a vocation. Why? Because in order to ignite the financial engine of your career, you need others to buy into what you are doing, whether they are fans, donors, granting organizations, arts presenters, schools, or students. Music designed only to please the maker is a wonderful hobby, but it does not set you up for making a living.

The good news is that you don't need an enormous audience to make a viable living. Making something people want doesn't mean that you must appeal to the lowest common denominator or go for mass appeal.

In reality, almost every authentic artistic voice can have an audience that is big enough to sustain it, although the process of finding that target audience may be trickier for some than for others. Fortunately, as described in Kevin Kelly's widely read article ("1000 True Fans"), you only really need one thousand true fans to make it happen.

It can take time to cultivate one thousand true fans, but it's not an unattainable goal. This means that it should be quite feasible to make music that appeals to an audience that is specific to you. The trick is widening your focus to include your target audience as a necessary component of your artistry. Again, this need not impact your creative process, but it does require a critical shift in mindset, and a willingness to take action on audience development.

Why Do We Like This Definition of Business?

We like this definition because it contains a formula for exchanging value coupled to an ongoing quest to find more people to whom we can provide that value.

It shifts our attention from selling to service. It is highly rewarding to be service-oriented. When an audience experiences the value we provide and is enriched and served by it, we, as the provider of that service, also have an incredibly rewarding experience. Moreover, it transforms a transactional experience into a relationship, one that involves deep emotion on both sides and, often, a desire to maintain the relationship.

In our experience, this approach to business provides a mutual feeling of gratitude. The audience appreciates having been served, or entertained, and, sometimes, even enlightened, and the performer appreciates the opportunity to have served and entertained. Moreover, audience appreciation for the unique artistry of the performer inspires and motivates us to give even more of ourselves in the future. In contrast to the joy of the performance itself, the financial compensation may even feel like an afterthought.

Doing business this way is very rewarding, so much so that we want more and more of it. We yearn to experience the audience connection and exchange of value—it almost feels wrong to think of it as "work."

An iCadenza Story

With this formula, we began offering individual consulting services through iCadenza. We truly love working with talented musicians and helping them to reach their goals.

After interviewing hundreds of musicians, we understood that there was a dearth of information about the skills needed to "make it" in music. However, there was a deeper issue as well. Even those who had the information to put themselves out there (in terms of understanding social media and other vehicles for promotion) didn't know what to say.

Many artists also felt a deep internal resistance to promoting themselves online. Some had other inhibitions preventing them from going after what they thought they wanted. Others just didn't know what they wanted and thought that there weren't any good options. Essentially, we met many dedicated, ambitious musicians who felt stuck and needed help getting to the next level.

While there were many common threads, each person was unique and required a unique approach. Most importantly, we found that many artists didn't want to feel so alone in the journey and wanted a supportive partner to encourage and guide them.

Our first consulting client was a wonderful singer and voice professor named Susan Kane. She had a burning desire to write a book to help singers make it in the world. Our task was to provide the support and encouragement, as well as the practical advice, she would need to make her book a reality. We were elated that Susan had put her faith in us, but also terrified. We were 23 and 24 years old and had little experience doing anything outside of academia, and certainly no experience shepherding someone's profession.

What we did have, though, was an understanding of the power of a neutral but supportive coaching presence, as we'd learned from working with life coaches ourselves. We also had a deepening knowledge of industry which we'd gained by doing so many interviews with music luminaries.

The work with Susan was transformative—for her, and for ourselves. Each session was a moment of magical synergy. We loved getting to know her, understanding her goals, and providing feedback and guidance each step of the way. It was the most fun "work" we'd ever done!

Working with Susan gave us the confidence to do more—to get to know different client stories, goals, and personalities. And, five years later, we've worked with nearly one hundred consulting clients, each unique and delightful in his or her own way.

Our deep work with clients resulted in the creation of our talent agency and artist management company, Cadenza Artists. It had never been part of our original game plan to start an agency. It happened because some of our consulting clients wanted us to represent them and actively help them find performance opportunities.

We had no idea how the agency world functioned. But, we were determined to learn. We were inspired and energized by the marvelous talent we were supporting in our consulting practice. It was a logical next step for us to want to do everything in our power to help our clients achieve the recognition and rewards we believed their talent so rightly deserved. Four and a half years later, Cadenza Artists has a staff of ten and a roster of over fifty artists in a variety of music, dance, and multi-disciplinary genres.

Our business is based on providing value to our clients. We love what we do, and our love is reflected in the service we provide.

Our professional life was born not from the desire to go into "business," but to play a meaningful role in the performing arts. Our role in this difficult and obstacle-filled world is to listen to our artists, to understand their needs and objectives, and to help them achieve the success to which they aspire. In the process, we have learned to listen to ourselves as well, to develop a business model that serves our role, and to understand that "business" is not alien to the arts but integral to the artist's success.

Putting It into Practice
Spend ten to fifteen minutes journaling on the following questions:

1. For whom are you making music?
2. How can you change your perspective so that you feel as though you're serving your audience? What value do you provide?
3. Listen to your audience. What's missing from their experience that you can provide?
4. How can you most effectively communicate to your audience?
5. How can you make a difference for your audience?

Chapter 4
Pillar #1: Know Who You Are

"Life isn't about finding yourself. Life is about creating yourself." - George Bernard Shaw

Getting to Know You: What Are You About?

Now that we've talked about what business is, and the attitudes and behaviors that you can develop to set yourself up for success, let's take a hard look at what it is that you're trying to do with your career.

First, you'll need to ask yourself some tough questions:

- What are you, as an artist and person, fundamentally about?
- What do you want more than anything?
- What is the burning desire that will always stay with you? We're not asking you to think of what you want to do with the rest of your life, and we're not asking how you're going to make your burning desire come true. Right now, we're asking you to listen in and get clear on what you deeply want and what's important to you.

Why is it so important to answer these questions? Because you've already signed up for a monumental task—pursuing a career in music-- which is not easy. If you're committed to this road, it is important that you are doing it for the right reasons. You need to know what motivates you to choose this path. In short, you must understand who you are because the music you produce is an expression of that. What qualities, desires, and beliefs are you expressing in your music?

Clarity of intention and heightened self-awareness are essential to your success. When you have contradictory intentions or lack clarity of purpose and destination, you are actually working against yourself. This can result in poor decision-making. Poor decisions can prolong your journey or derail you entirely.

Your burning desire doesn't require a clear action plan or even a name. And, this desire might take the form of an impression you are trying to create, or a feeling you are seeking to convey, or evoke, even if you don't yet know how it will be achieved.

For us, as we were starting our companies, we really had a tough time connecting with our burning desire. We wanted to make something happen, and there was a lot of drive and passion, but we were so hung up on *how* we were going to succeed, and *how* we would make our dreams a reality, that we didn't spend enough time on *what* it was that we truly wanted to create.

Why was this a struggle? Mostly because of fear. We were afraid of taking our foot off of the gas petal and braking long enough to listen to our inner dialogues. We were afraid that if we slowed our momentum and stopped taking action, our engine would fail and not turn on again. We thought that action was the only way to accelerate, and didn't give our thoughts and intentions enough weight.

It wasn't until we paused long enough to honor our passion and connect with the fire in our bellies, that we started to see things take shape.

Think about hiking on an unfamiliar trail. Although the trail is new, you envision your destination at the summit, even though the hike is really about the experience. You haven't planned your hike in detail—you don't know whether you'll go left or right when you hit a fork in the road. Is going left going to be more difficult? Steeper? What if there's a dead end?

Somehow, you trust that when you encounter that fork in the road, you'll figure it out. As you proceed, you navigate all sorts of terrain. If you make a wrong call, you might have to retrace some of your steps. But eventually, you make it to the top—victory!

Now, imagine how much more difficult it would have been to get to the summit if you weren't totally sure of your destination. What would have happened if you had been motivated by two conflicting desires: making it to the top, versus heading toward the bottom of an adjacent ravine? What if you had tried to decide beforehand that, whenever you came to a fork, you'd go left—without even knowing where left would take you?

By the time you make it to the top or to the bottom, you wouldn't know whether you had succeeded or failed because you hadn't been clear about your objective at the outset.

When you are encumbered with conflicting intentions, succeeding at one, by definition, means failing at the other. Consider the performing artist who passionately desires a stable family life with minimal travel, who also wants a vibrant solo career requiring constant travel. If you opt for one you are, in the logical world, saying "no" to the other. We are firm believers that you *can* have it all, but when you have competing desires, you can't have them all *at once.* So you have to choose.

So what is it that you truly want? When are you happiest? What gives you the most fulfillment?

Embracing Your Passion

Once you know your passion, that's when the hard part begins. You need to fully embrace it.

Julia's Story

For me, embracing my passion has always been a tough pill to swallow. My deepest joy is knowing that I'm helping others realize their potential, working with people, and creating an environment in which I, and others, can thrive.

I also know that financial stability and ample time at home with family are important to me. As soon as I put those things out there, my knee-jerk reaction is to judge them.

Without skipping a beat, that critical voice inside me jumps up and starts pushing my buttons:

Who made me so high and mighty that I think I can help others?

I haven't even realized my potential yet—and probably never will.

And don't I think that wanting financial stability is selfish? So is time with family. There's no way that I can have that if I really want to excel in my career.

What will others think of me if I say these things? They will think that I'm an elitist snob with a superiority complex. Definitely.

At this point, the trick is to resist believing your inner critic. Allow yourself to truly embrace your passion and the ideal vision for your lifestyle. Recognize that you're not perfect, that you're just doing the best that you can, and that you are deeply committed to making what you want a reality. Tell that voice "thanks for sharing" and don't buy into its negativity.

Accepting and embracing your passion—the activities that fill you with joy and allow you to thrive—is critically important, not just to ensure success in creating the passion in the long run, but also to give you direction and permission to take action in the short-term.

For me, there are days when I soar and get an extraordinary amount accomplished. And there are other days when I feel as though the entire day is a struggle against time, and full of obstacles.

I've noticed that the days when I am most "on," most effective, and most focused have little to do with what happens to me or even with how I feel about things that happen to me. Instead, in my experience, the difference on those days is how I'm feeling about myself and how accepting I am of myself and what I stand for. For me, it makes all the difference.

Jim's Story

A couple of years ago, we had the privilege of working with Jim, a talented pianist living in a small town. For many years, Jim struggled to believe in himself, accepting sub-par opportunities for too-low fees. He was overworked and wasn't getting the kinds of jobs that fulfilled him.

Jim wondered if he was simply not destined to succeed. He wondered whether he was good enough.

At the beginning of his career, he had received a lot of harsh feedback from teachers and critics, and, internalizing the negativity, he had decided against the possibility of success very early on. He felt alone in his struggle. To numb the pain, he created a barrier between himself and his emotions. But that barrier also separated him from his heartfelt thoughts and desires.

Our work consisted of helping him unravel the judgment that he had internalized, and of dispelling the cruel voices in his head that were so destructive to his confidence. We encouraged him to shift his thinking and to replace the judgment with positive, affirming messages. We also worked through a number of exercises to help Jim clarify his mission statement and true aspirations.

The results of this work affected every area of Jim's life. For the first time, he was able to view his failures and successes with objectivity. Most importantly, he was able to banish his unbalanced attachment to his failures.

He realized that many of the gigs that he had been accepting, and which paid very little, did not reflect his true ambitions. They were diversions that kept him from pursuing the engagements that he really wanted. Previously, he had believed that he did not have the luxury to decline any opportunity. He did not have the emotional tools to evaluate an offer in terms of its suitability for his career path. With his new clarity, Jim began declining longstanding, reliable gigs that just weren't right for him.

As an unexpected bonus, Jim reported that even his piano practice improved. It became more joyful, and, therefore, more effective. For the first time in decades, his music was not just about self-validation, and self-justification. It was about creating something that shared joy, meaning and inspiration.

Jim also realized that he had many people in his camp who were rooting for his success. Donors, collaborators, and cheerleaders in his network appeared very quickly, and he was able to create new projects and start to develop mini-tours to perform them. He began to organize local concerts that were in line with his passions. Suddenly, opportunities materialized.

"The Journey of a Thousand Miles Begins with One Step" - Lao Tzu

Jim's story illustrates the power of accepting our own heartfelt hopes and dreams.

Now, we turn back to you. Once you've embraced your passion, it's time to start living it out and making it a reality. However, the pressure to do the "right thing," especially once you're deeply connected with your passion, can be overwhelming.

It's refreshing to recognize that life only requires one tiny step after another, and one tiny decision after another. Whether you know exactly what you're building or whether you only have an idea for one aspect of it, you're still going to have to lay the foundation brick by brick.

Putting It into Practice:

If you, like many of us, feel unsure about who you are and what you want, we encourage you to spend five to ten minutes writing out responses to each of the questions below in your journal. The act of putting your thoughts into words can often bring out ideas that you didn't realize were there!

1. What experiences stand out as the most rewarding and memorable to you?
2. What do you value most?
3. Create your "Living Vision." Picture your ideal day six months in the future and write about it in the present tense. This is your moment to dream big! We encourage you to have a stretch vision—something that is fifty percent believable and fifty percent unbelievable.

Getting into Action

Now that you've done the hard part, it's time to have fun. We encourage you to view this part of the process as an experiment, and approach it from a playful perspective. This is a game, and the objective is to identify and/or create a job that is in line with your burning passion.

How can you move towards your passion in a manner that delivers value to others? Remember that there is an immense diversity of job opportunities for any musician.

In addition to solo and ensemble opportunities through established channels, you can start your own series, sell online products and services, start a teaching studio on your own terms, work with executives on how they can unleash their creativity, write a book about your professional journey for aspiring musicians...the list is endless.

Your creativity is the limit here. If you're creating something that doesn't exist, the best way to determine how to build it is to get into conversation with people and really listen to their needs. Take an informal survey of people around you and identify trends. When you see an overlap between a service or product that people want, a skill set that you have, and your passion, you have hit the jackpot. Your passion-laden business project is born.

To access our Mission Statement Exercise, and other free extras, be sure to check out **http://www.icadenza.com/ebook-resources/**

Chapter 5
Pillar #2: Adopt a Positive Mindset

"If we make up our minds that this is a drab and purposeless universe, it will be that, and nothing else. On the other hand, if we believe that the earth is ours, and that the sun and moon hang in the sky for our delight, there will be joy upon the hills and gladness in the fields because the Artist in our souls glorifies creation. Surely, it gives dignity to life to believe that we are born into this world for noble ends, and that we have a higher destiny than can be accomplished within the narrow limits of this physical life." - Helen Keller

Once we delve into and articulate our motivations, dreams, and vision, we need to peer into the environment they inhabit within us. If our dreams and goals are flowers, their ability to grow depends on the quality of the soil. The "soil" is your mind—the internal environment you create to support your dreams. Are you creating an internal environment that enables your dreams to thrive and become real, or is the soil hostile to them?

A career in music can be an exercise in emotional vulnerability. Rejection, gigs falling through, insufficient funds, a diminishing audience for classical repertoire, unsupportive family members, critical reviews, and other let-downs, all take their toll on the artist's psyche.

With heartbreak and disappointment always (potentially) around the corner, how do we maintain a spirit of confidence and optimism? How do we create an environment within our own minds that is supportive and nurturing, in the face of relentless challenges?

Musicians are experts at uncovering defects, and pointing them out. They also like to try to fix them. But a narrow focus on what's wrong can lead to a mindset of skepticism and cynicism, justified by the belief of, "well, that's the reality."

A core tenet in our work is optimism. We strive to instill, in ourselves and our clients, a positive view of the future in order to create our desired destiny. A common response we'll hear is, "Yes, but that's ignoring the reality of the situation."

To promote optimism is not to deny reality but rather to project your intentions onto reality. We understand that, although life can throw us a curve ball, and that much is beyond our control, we must confidently claim the driver's seat, and steer our career away from the valleys and toward the hills. In other word, seek out the future you want, even if it seems so far away.

Where's Your Mind?

Every self-help book today proclaims that we manifest what we envision. But, there seems to be a practical basis for this assertion. Social scientists have identified a human phenomenon called confirmation bias—the tendency to seek out andinterpret information in a way that confirms one's beliefs. Essentially, we all like to be right. If we hold certain beliefs, we tend to look for validation to confirm they are true. Even when faced with evidence to the contrary, we may not notice it.

Let's do a thought experiment: do you believe people are generous and eager to help you, or do you believe that people are selfish and will take advantage of you whenever they have the chance?

Let's pretend Charlie is a musician who believes that people are selfish and prone to take advantage of him. He's driving down the road and gets cut off. Though he may not have an outburst, on the inside he thinks "I can't believe people in this town! Everyone is so rude!" At the supermarket, he can't find a clerk to help him. When he finally finds someone and asks (perhaps with a little bit of frustration) where the cereal is, the clerk answers quickly and scurries away.

Charlie is frustrated with where he is career-wise and wishes that people in the "right places" would help him. But his attempts at networking with people who might help him haven't led to anything. No one seems to want to help, so why bother to ask? He knows that he is a great musician but there just aren't any opportunities these days, so why should he spend more time hustling (which he hates anyway) if it doesn't work?

Now, let's take Emily, and imagine that she believes that people are generous and eager to help her. When she goes to the supermarket, she smiles and is friendly to others. She has found that, most of the time, when she smiles at someone, that person smiles back.

When she asks the clerk for help, he responds warmly and points her in the right direction. She loves connecting with people, even if only for a brief moment with a stranger. Sometimes, someone cuts in front of her when she is driving. Her usual reaction is, "Yikes! Something must be going on with that person. I'm glad I reacted in time!" but she doesn't think much of it once the incident has passed.

When it comes to networking and growing her career, Emily has an attitude of, "It never hurts to ask." In her experience, people are often surprisingly generous when she approaches them. Therefore, she pushes herself to reach out to people in order to see if there is synergy. "The worst that could happen is that someone might say no."

Obviously these examples are simplistic. But the point is that our outlook fundamentally affects how we perceive the world. Our attitude even affects what we choose to remember and what we choose to forget. Charlie's expectation that he will be disappointed causes him to go into situations on the lookout for confirmation of his belief that no one is on his side. Not only does this affect his quality of life, it affects his willingness to take action to advance his goals because he wonders, "What's the point?"

Moreover, the people that he encounters might sense his frustration, and be repelled by it. The clerk at the supermarket sees Charlie's upset face, which he reads as anger, and wants to avoid it. People in a position to help him with his career might sense Charlie's negativity and prefer to move on, as well.

Emily's mindset, on the other hand, enables her to find small moments of joy in her daily life as she connects with people over the little things. If something annoys or frustrates her, she lets it go because stuff happens—it doesn't mean the world is out to get her. Her "Why not try?" attitude gives her permission to put out feelers on the off-chance that something positive might come back, even though there is no guarantee. Her positivity and friendly demeanor help ensure that people actually look forward to interacting with her.

The big question is, do you believe the world is a hospitable environment for you and your dreams? Or do you believe the world is a hostile environment for your dreams?

So, ask yourself: within your mind and thoughts, are you creating a hospitable environment for your dreams, or are you creating a hostile one?

Roadblocks to Optimism

Obviously, you can't just wish yourself to be more optimistic. A change in mindset doesn't happen overnight. Sometimes, when you open yourself to a new way of thinking, your old patterns rear up even more powerfully than before, as though they are determined to survive.

There are two thought patterns that are particularly detrimental to a positive outlook: judgment and negative fantasies. Let's explore each of these in turn. You'll learn how they manifest so you can be on the lookout for these thoughts. Awareness is the necessary first step in order to change.

Judgment: An Overblown Focus on Others

We love to judge. Therefore, we give judgment major status in our minds. From sarcastic humor to making fun of how other people dress, talk, or do just about anything, it's easy to judge others. Some people judge others but reserve no criticism for themselves. And many judge themselves even more harshly than they judge others.

Whatever the case, judgment rarely leads to the peace of mind necessary to promote an optimistic outlook. Judgment places an unhealthy emphasis on other people rather than on ourselves. Often times, as we judge others, we judge ourselves *in comparison* to others. Judgment takes up valuable mental space that could be dedicated to productive, optimistic thought. As we will discuss, an antidote to a habitual focus on judgment can be to focus deliberately on intentions.

Amy's Story

We observed our client, Amy, cycle through various stages of judgment as she worked through obstacles preventing her from starting a blog.

We admired her honesty and self-awareness when she admitted that while she believed that writing about her artistry required vulnerability, she felt uncomfortable exposing her flaws. She fretted that she would appear too touchy-feely and insubstantial as a person. Even though she acknowledged that she *is* someone who likes to talk about feelings and believes in positive psychology, she judged other musicians who blogged about their inner struggles. Do you see how she was judging others, judging herself, and judging others for how they might judge her? That's a lot of mental energy spent on judgment!

We highlight this example because of how completely normal it is. We were grateful to Amy for sharing her mental process with us, with all of its twists and turns, The more we can be mindful of our thought patterns, the better our chance at making space for more productive thoughts.

Negative Fantasies

It is a real challenge to be optimistic when confronted with stressful or high-stakes situations. When you prepare for a recital or go into an interview, the brain can easily dwell on the worst possibilities. "I'll forget the words, my voice will crack, I'll trip and fall." "I'll say something stupid, he will be really intimidating, he'll ask me a question I don't know how to answer."

Think about the physical impact of these thought patterns. They might cause your heart to race, your stomach to churn. Maybe your hands become cold, your breathing becomes shallow. You might start sweating. Our bodies translate our mental state into a physical reaction that is theoretically supposed to prepare us for the impending crisis. The result of our unwanted physical responses to stress, however, is reduced oxygen to our brain, which impairs thinking. So, in the very moment that you need your brain to function optimally, it is compromised by your temporary state of stressed-induced panic.

While it may be difficult to completely calm the nerves before an important moment, we can minimize this effect significantly by being deliberate about our thoughts. Do you allow the negative fantasies to spin out of control? Or, do you direct the conversation in your head by creating a positive intention for the experience and outcome of the event?

We highly recommend the practice of visualizing the event unfolding in the precise manner that you desire, with the most positive outcome. Many music teachers recommend this technique when it comes to preparing for a performance, but it can be applied just as effectively to meetings, auditions, networking events, and any other looming experience that brings you anxiety.

Making the Case for Optimism

Our minds are easily programmable. Whatever messages we repeat to ourselves and visualize often enough, we start to believe over time. Therefore, we are better off if the messages we transmit to ourselves are positive ones. We highly recommend creating deliberate affirmations and making time to visualize them so that you can ultimately adopt new beliefs. State the positive affirmations aloud to root them into your psyche. As awkward as it may feel, engaging multiple senses in the process makes a big difference.

Most importantly, an optimistic outlook applied specifically to your unique dream is an unstoppable combination. If you focus on your desire to create your dream, and work to ingrain in your mind the belief that you can do it, then you will eventually act in a manner that is consistent with your goals. There are countless examples of people who defied the odds, and achieved something that others said was impossible. To become one of those people, you must create an internal environment of optimism and belief that your vision can become a reality.

An Unexpected Client

Most clients come to us with a general idea of where they want to go. Along the way, we coach them through the process of clarifying and achieving their goals and help set them up for success.

Not long ago, we had the opportunity to meet Greg Sandow, a composer, writer, teacher, consultant, and thought leader for people concerned with the future of classical music.

We discussed a host of things—his work, our work, his and our ideas about the future of the industry and what excites us most. Greg exudes an unstoppable optimism in everything he does. He has a broad vision of how the classical music industry can successfully reach new audiences— and how he can help.

The next day, something unusual happened. Greg sent us an email saying that he would like to work with us, and sent us a proposal. It reflected exceptional clarity of vision, and was premised on his belief that he could reach more people with his work, and feel more fulfilled doing it. He thought that achieving this goal was not only possible, but inevitable. He enlisted our support to make the proposal a reality.

Our work together will succeed because Greg has a track record of success due to his unstoppable optimism and open-mindedness. This optimism feeds his willingness to act. He is open to growth and learning and is biased toward action.

From the get-go, we've been impressed with Greg's attitude towards our work together. Our impression is that he approaches it with the commitment that it will be successful, rather than constantly questioning whether it will have been worthwhile. In our view, this attitude of certainty is a predictor of his success. Greg's commitment to a successful outcome (combined with ours) will ensure that that will be the result. His is a winning attitude, both in the short- and long-term.

Putting It into Practice

Now that you have worked on the questions of who you are and what you want most, it's time to invest in a mindset that will support you in achieving your goals. We encourage you to do the following:

1.   Remember the Living Vision you created about a positive day in your future? We encourage you to read that at least once a day. Feel free to update and modify it as your ideas expand.

2.   Spend five minutes creating a brief statement that encapsulates your vision, which you can read aloud to yourself every morning and night. It is important to read it aloud so that you engage both your eyes

and ears with this important message. This is similar to the Living Vision exercise but more condensed—this is designed to be your daily affirmation.

3.   Spend five minutes journaling every day for the next week to track your mindset. Do you ever find yourself sliding into judgment? Have you had any negative fantasies? When you pay attention to your thought patterns, what do you notice?

4.   As you develop greater awareness about your thought patterns, try to identify opportunities to assume a new outlook, one that is more supportive of your goals.

Chapter 6
Pillar #3: Enroll Others in Your Vision

Once you've discerned what you're really about and embraced a positive attitude, you can consider how others fit into your vision. We need the support of others, their participation, feedback, and buy-in. It's hard to create in a vacuum and you certainly can't create *for* a vacuum. This chapter is all about relationship-building and leadership.

Relationships

Our world is more technology-centered than ever before. We interact through email, often without ever meeting the person on the other end. We send in our audition recordings by uploading files to a website. We write to thousands of fans by entering 140 characters of text and clicking a button.

It's important to remember, however, that while the channels through which we communicate have evolved, we are still communicating with other *people*. The people on the other end are human beings, with their own dreams as well as their own fears, challenges, and obstacles. Sometimes, we are so absorbed in our own issues that we forget about the person on the other side.

The people on the other side may be professionals in the field. They may be in the process of deciding your fate by choosing the performers in their series this year. They may be aiming for objectivity in their selection of artists who are vying for gigs. Still, never forget that they are human beings having a human experience. And a human experience consists of many relationships.

Your ability to develop meaningful relationships with people will determine the course of your career. In the pages that follow, we will share three tips to help you succeed in building strong relationships with presenters, financial supporters, collaborators, students (and their parents), and anyone else with whom you desire to be connected on a personal or professional level. Later in this chapter, we'll suggest immediate steps you can take to develop and maintain deeper relationships.

Tip #1: Be Genuinely Interested in the Thoughts of Others

People seldom remember what others say to them, but they almost always remember how others made them feel. If people remember feeling heard, valued, and important when they interact with you, they will welcome future interactions and regard you with greater interest.

The key is to be genuinely curious and interested in their thoughts. Learn to listen attentively, and avoid interrupting in mid-sentence. When interacting with those who have the power to offer you work, seek to know the factors at play with regard to programming decisions. Demonstrate an understanding of the inherent frustrations in deciding between worthy performers. Inquire about past successes. What do they strive for in their productions?

Are you willing to ask questions so that you can learn what matters to them? To do so requires you to momentarily put your own needs and interests aside.

Tip #2: Be Prepared to Ask for What You Want

While we advise you to engage others with sensitivity, curiosity and attentiveness, never lose sight of your own goals. Still, relationship-building in the music industry serves an end in itself, and one relationship can lead to others. Not all relationships will bear fruit. But some, if not many, will.

Moreover, developing a relationship—by engaging others with sensitivity, curiosity and attentiveness--opens the door for you to communicate your goals and visions. Your own listening skills will tell you when the opportunity has presented itself. Once you speak up, share your vision in a succinct manner and be prepared to ask for what you want.

Tip #3: Keep Tabs on People and Follow Up

The curiosity we recommended in Tip #1, may have resulted in the disclosure to you of personal information that could give you an opportunity to follow up in the near future. Beyond your interest in obtaining gigs, constantly look for opportunities to deepen a relationship in a genuine way. We can only advise that you be guided by your best instincts in blurring the line between personal and professional communications.

Keep track of details that enable follow-up communications, which can prove valuable months or even years later. For example, if someone tells you about a new project or series they will be launching in the future, you then have the opportunity to inquire about it from time to time.

As simple as it sounds, you can never go wrong by remembering a birthday. It is a great opportunity to show your interest and care on a personal level. Not only does it put a smile on the recipient's face, but in some cases it might remind that person that he or she had been meaning to reach out to you!

What Penguins Teach Us about Leadership

Recently, our agency and the conductor we represent, Jeffrey Schindler, produced the presentation of the Academy Award-winning film, *March of the Penguins,* live with music performed by the Seattle Symphony.

March of the Penguins is a documentary that describes Antarctica's emperor penguins' annual saga to mate and raise their young. The mother and father penguins alternate between keeping the egg, and subsequently the chick, warm while the other parent walks more than seventy miles to the ocean's edge in search of food. Each foray takes many weeks.

It is a story of survival against all odds in "the harshest place on earth," where temperatures regularly drop as low as -125° Fahrenheit!

Each march toward the ocean for food requires a change in route; new environmental obstacles keep emerging along the way. The film observes the role of leadership as well as group mentality in the penguins' journey toward the ocean for food— the key to their survival.

During the 70+ mile trek in the freezing cold, they march relentlessly, single file, often day and night, to their destination. They keep moving to make it back in time with food so that their young don't die, stopping only occasionally for a brief respite.

When they are confronted with an obstacle, their progress comes to an abrupt halt. They loiter helplessly in place. Then, the miracle occurs. One penguin emerges as the leader. She overcomes the obstacle by changing direction. The others look, watch and wait as she puts distance between herself and them. Hesitant at first, they begin to follow the first penguin into the unknown. That penguin became the new leader.

What Does It Mean to Be a Leader?

A leader is someone who is able to communicate a vision, establish a direction and a strategy to achieve it, and enlist others to join him on a quest they might not otherwise have elected to undertake.

In many ways, leadership is about influence. You are presenting or modeling an alternative way of doing something and offering others the chance to come along with you on the journey.

In order for it to be effective, leadership has to begin with you and your mindset. As we discussed in chapters 4 and 5, you have to be willing to stand up for what you believe, and you need to be willing to adopt a positive mindset around that goal. When you do this, by definition, you're challenging the status quo in some capacity—if you weren't, you wouldn't be leading, you'd be following.

To be a leader is to voluntarily place yourself in an awkward and lonely position: there is a gap between the moment that you declare your vision and the time that others are convinced to follow you. During that space, you will be on your own without support from others.

Without approval from others, you might, understandably, question whether you're doing the right thing. You may begin to doubt your vision as well as yourself. You've taken a big risk. Should you stick with it, or should you backtrack and rejoin the fold?

Sticking with it means getting up in the morning every day and putting one foot in front of the other, living out your passion proudly, and never forgetting your vision, even when you get doors slammed in your face.

We'll give you a few tangible examples of how this works.

Perhaps you've heard of Dancing Guy, as presented by Derek Sivers, who is an accomplished entrepreneur, writer, and mover and shaker in the music industry. Among other achievements, he founded CDBaby. Dancing Guy is a video that Derek narrated to demonstrate how leadership works. Watch it by searching YouTube for "First Follower: Leadership Lessons from Dancing Guy."

Without a doubt, Apple is a major leader in technology. Their products have fundamentally changed how we communicate, listen to music, and relate to technology in general. Their leadership and product designers envision a future that is far beyond what the average consumer could predict.

Examples of trail blazers in music and art are countless. The great composers, musicians, and other artists were and are innovators who dared to challenge the status quo by pushing the edge of what was understood to be the norm.

Stravinsky, Van Gogh, Handel, and in more recent times, The Beatles, Madonna, and Lady Gaga—they all challenged convention and did something totally different, and were not necessarily accepted at first.

The point here is not to think of something radical to do just for the sake of doing something radical. Lasting, effective leadership only works if you fully buy into your idea, with passion and commitment.

It's not about challenging convention and getting wrapped up in the debate. It's about stepping out of the crowd and dancing to your heart's content, like the Dancing Guy, doing what you are passionate about, and being willing to do it for long enough and visibly enough for others to want to join in.

Once you've developed the mindset to keep you in the game for the long haul, you need to make sure that you establish the environment that keeps others in your corner as well.

Putting It into Practice

Take some time to complete the following:

1. Create a list of people whom you know or with whom you have worked, who are fans of your work and might be willing to open a door for you, serve as a reference, or give you a helpful suggestion.

2. Create another list of people whom you'd like to get to know or with whom you would like to connect. Given the opportunity to connect with them, what would you say or ask? Some of the people on this list might be in the "stretch" category. These are people that you can't easily envision a way to reach. It's good to have a fair number of people in that "stretch" category on your list.

3. Create a schedule for how you will maintain your existing relationships with all the people on list one as well as how you plan to connect with some of the people on list two. For the latter, consider: who do you know who might know each of those people? As far as the schedule is concerned, we suggest reaching out to people, at least through email, every four to six months to stay in touch and to keep your name present in their minds.

4. To practice leadership, think of an area where you can test out being the "lone dancer." What are opportunities for you to practice being uncomfortable while standing up for something that truly matters to you?

Chapter 7
Pillar #4: Understand the Art of Negotiation

Tug of War

One of the words artists fear the most is "negotiation." The word invokes thoughts of battle and confrontation. Unfortunately, artists usually expect to be trampled--meaning that they fear being taken advantage of, or being handed a bad deal. We understand why you might feel that way. We experienced these fears ourselves when we started our business. However, we want to present to you a radically different approach.

First, let's recognize that we all negotiate every single day. Life is really a series of negotiations, whether we are negotiating in a business setting or with family and friends regarding personal issues, preferences, plans and opportunities.

The practice of negotiation is not limited to contracts and money. In our business, we negotiate relationships on a constant basis.

We negotiate with venues on behalf of the artists we represent, and we negotiate with clients about how our relationship will be structured.

We also negotiate with our artists over how we will achieve our common goals. We work with prospective clients to negotiate realistic expectations and deliverables.

We negotiate with our staff on how to accomplish the goals we set for our business. Each person is an advocate for the ideas he or she brings to the table. The process of strategy-selection among capable individuals requires negotiation. We also negotiate over our business priorities. Like any thriving business, we have many irons in the fire. Opportunities, obligations, and commitments demand that we also negotiate with ourselves over which project or strategy should take priority at any given moment.

The two of us, by nature, tend to be non-confrontational. Therefore, if we viewed negotiation as a combative, challenging, scary, zero-sum game, we'd be pretty miserable. Fortunately, with the help of our own coaches, we found a way to relate to negotiation that is much more positive and productive.

What Is Negotiation?

Negotiation is a process leading to an exchange of value for each participant. The agreed terms of the exchange constitute a deal. Value can be a wonderful performance at your venue. It can be money. It can be a free practice space.

You can be creative in thinking of the ways to acquire value as a result of negotiation. For performers, the exchange usually involves a performance in exchange for a fee.

First we will analyze what's really happening when an exchange for performance is made, and then we'll talk about how to determine whether a given exchange is in line with what you seek. Finally, we'll discuss how to negotiate from a position of power.

Values Exchange

Normally, when an artist receives compensation, he or she sees it as a reflection of the value of his time: "How much is my time worth?"

Sometimes, the question becomes: "How much am I worth?" Thus, the transaction becomes very personal. If I get paid one thousand dollars to sing a recital, am I really worth one thousand dollars per night?

I received an offer to sing at a friend's wedding for two hundred dollars. Does this mean I am being valued at two hundred dollars? If I say yes, am I agreeing that I'm only worth two hundred dollars for a performance?

When you negotiate an agreement, you may feel that you are giving your services away to a bargain hunter.

Instead, we prefer to see compensation more dispassionately. It's just a values exchange. Each party is giving away something in exchange for value. You have artistic abilities. The other party has money. You decide what kind of service you can provide, and what kind of monetary compensation you are looking for that the other party can provide. This does not have to be a judgment about your self-worth and should not be.

When to Say Yes to a Values Exchange and When to Say No

How do you know when the values exchange is appropriate? What is the "right" amount of money?

The answers to these questions depend on two factors. We'll break them down for you below, but first, just a quick note.

The discussion in this chapter is all about values exchange and negotiation, but we're making an assumption that you're keeping chapter 4 in mind. If an opportunity just isn't in line with your passion and mission statement, no amount of negotiation will help make it "fit."

Before you get to the negotiating table, you need to decide whether or not the opportunity presenting itself aligns with your goals and principles. If the answer is "no," then it's probably not a good idea to pursue it further.

Now, let us turn to the two factors that we should consider when determining the "right" amount of money in a given values exchange.

Factor #1: Have a Sense of the Market Price

It's important to know the range that others charge for a similar service. If you are offering something totally unique, and nobody is doing anything similar, try to identify an analogous industry in order to come up with a ballpark estimate. If others do offer what you're offering, then just ask around. There's nothing wrong with approaching a competitor and asking him or her what is normally charged.

Sometimes, conversations about money can feel awkward, and, therefore, we are reluctant to ask the crucial question about the fee. However, if you are willing to share the answer to the same question when it is asked of you, then almost any question is fair game.

We are not recommending that you restrict yourself to the average price range that others are demanding for their services. It's just good to know whether you are the most expensive act in town, or whether your rates are below market.

Some people actually equate value with cost, and believe that a service or an object that costs more is actually better. This can work to your advantage if you are, in fact, the most expensive service-provider in your area. But, this research will also inform you if you're undercharging. Unless you're still committed to the starving artist mentality (and if so, please reread chapters 2 and 3, or email us at jennifer@icadenza.com!), there is no reason to be undercharging.

Factor #2: Ask for What Inspires You

The second and more important factor that will help you determine the "right" amount of money to ask for begins with this question: "What amount of money will I need to receive that will enable me to bring my A game to this job?"

This question addresses a fear common to many artists: they do not want to be seen as greedy or asking for too much. But, you need money to survive. You have a certain minimum threshold amount that you need each month to cover your bills and living expenses.

Covering those costs might require you to accept a variety of performance opportunities— some that you passionately want to do, and some that you are simply willing to do. However, if a job leaves you cold, or doesn't fit your mission statement, as we discussed in chapter 4, perhaps you should label it a distraction, pass on the opportunity, and move on.

If you are offered an inadequate fee for a given service, consider whether you will be able to bring your A game to the job, or whether resentment will hinder your ability to perform. If you're sitting in hours of traffic on the way to the gig and thinking, "Why did I accept this? I'm not even getting paid enough to cover the gas money," then it is going to be difficult to truly give your best on the stage. If an opportunity puts you at a loss financially, requires you to take on even more work, or to put in more hours at the day job to make ends meet, *and* your internal dialogue related to the project is not one of joy and excitement, then it is better to say no.

It's important to remember that every gig or service has costs that can be quantified, whether they are expenses like gas or contracting other musicians, or the cost of your time. Make sure to know those costs before you quote or accept a fee, so that you are making an informed decision that sets you up for success.

This is fair reasoning, and you can even share it with the person with whom you are negotiating. "I understand that you're saying that your budget is X, but for me to be able to do my best work, I'll need to turn down other opportunities to make sure that I put in sufficient time for this project. In order to make that feasible, I need a minimum budget of Y. How can we get creative to make that possible?"

We want to share a story about our client Cathy. Several years ago, she accepted an opera role with a very small opera company. The job paid very little but it was a role that she wanted for her résumé. Not considering the values exchange, and stuck in a mindset of scarcity, she felt that she needed to accept the gig for lack of better alternatives.

The rehearsals and performances were about two hours away from where she lived, plus the job required a monthlong commitment, with rehearsals five days a week, several hours each day. As the performance dates approached, she was committed to a tech week of daily rehearsals, followed by a run of four performances. The compensation she was receiving barely covered the rising gas costs to fuel her car.

She related this story to us, and expressed her pain. She felt as though she'd given herself away and that she had been used for the advantage of others, with little or no reward for herself. She had lost much time and energy fulfilling her end of the bargain, yet received little in return. As a result, she was tired and demoralized.

She had been forced to carry a full load of teaching and other jobs during that month because the money for the role just wasn't enough. And, while she made it through, she had not been able to bring her A game to the experience and certainly did not enjoy it.

When you aren't able to produce your best, you disappoint yourself, and possibly your audience. Besides, you never know who is watching you perform: future employers, reporters, and other influential people, all of whom come to see excellent work. Furthermore, consider the damage to your own creativity when you place yourself in a position of resentment and exhaustion associated with your art.

And, of course, there's the issue of "opportunity cost." If you hadn't accepted a job that does not serve you, would something better have come along?

Does No Mean Never?

If, after you have considered the factors above, you realize that your answer is "no," your conversation with the person who offered you the job doesn't need to be dramatic. You are not rejecting that person or his or her project. The job is just not the right fit for you at this time.

You can say "no" respectfully. Everything in this business depends on relationships, and whether your answer is "yes" or "no," you are building a relationship with that person.

Can you say "no" in a way that will encourage this person to call you when he or she has a future project? Can your interaction build up the relationship rather than tear it down? Be tactful, and clear so as to assure him or her that you are not leaving anyone in the lurch by not accepting an offer at this time.

It's totally possible that in a few years, this person will be at a new organization or will have a new project that's perfectly in line with what you're hoping to do. You never know! This has happened to us many times.

In short, remember that saying "no" to the situation does not have to mean saying "no" to the person and to the relationship.

Entering the Battlefield

So what do you do when your answer isn't "no" but you need to work with the person you're negotiating with to get onto the same page?

It is fascinating that in most negotiations, people often think that they are fighting for power. "If I give in on this, I will be perceived as weak," or, "If I take a friendlier tone, they will walk all over me," or conversely, "If I stand up for what is important to me, I will be viewed as aggressive."

Stuck in a power struggle, you can sometimes forget what you're negotiating for in the first place. And, amazingly, if you're willing to let go of the power dynamics and actually listen to the other person's interests and concerns, you may find that it's not a zero-sum game. It's also completely possible—even likely—that you might arrive at a solution where you both get what you want.

In Julia's master's program, Professors Craig and Linda Barkacs taught the concept of "pie expansion" in negotiations. Imagine a metaphorical pie. In negotiations, people often feel that their objective is to try to get a bigger piece, so that the other person gets a smaller piece. Sometimes, people even think that only one of the two negotiators can walk away with the pie. That's what's called a zero-sum situation—if I win, you lose, and vice versa. But in reality, if you think creatively, it's totally possible that you can grow the actual pie so that everyone walks away with more.

For example, if two companies are competing for the same small set of customers, they could instead work together to grow the total number of customers. For instance, by advertising to a new demographic, or rolling out a set of products to appeal to a broader customer base, the two competitors can both grow their companies. But to do this, each needs to be willing to not be the "winner." They will both win much more if they decide that they are willing to work together, instead of against one another.

How to Handle a Challenging Negotiating Partner

Sometimes, the person you're negotiating with is stuck in his or her own power struggle. When you hear that in their voice or see it in their body language, it is tempting to react in kind.

Over the years, we've learned to quickly notice that inclination within ourselves. So, we take a deep breath, and choose to say no to that urge. When you refuse to yell back when someone is yelling at you, eventually, the other person will see that you're not willing to engage in a tense power struggle, and will appreciate your commitment to the actual issue at hand.

Sometimes, the person you're negotiating with doesn't actually have strong opinions about his or her position—only a desire to be heard and respected. Sometimes, when he or she knows that you really listened and that you care about and empathize with his or her goals and concerns, that person will be more disposed to tilt the scales in your favor. In this situation, it can be helpful to just let the other person get it all out. Once a person releases all the bottled-up thoughts and energy, he or she is usually in a more rational and productive place to have a real conversation. Your creativity will allow both of you to develop new ideas to your mutual benefit.

Growing the Pie

You can get into a "pie expansion" conversation by hitting the pause button, and listening to the other person's needs carefully, and with empathy. Then, you consider the other person's needs and wants and measure how they stack up against yours. If you say yes to what the other person wants, are you saying no to what you want? If so, how can you act creatively to achieve your goal?

What if your priorities are not compromised by agreeing to what your negotiating partner wants? Can you say yes and then share what you are looking for? You may feel that you are backing down. You may feel as though you're giving away your power. If so, perhaps you are stuck in the "me versus them" mindset—a broken record that says, if they win, I lose. And nobody wants to lose.

However, the fact that you've engaged in a productive discussion to facilitate mutual understanding is relationship-building in itself. Demonstrating goodwill during a negotiation is essential when you expect to negotiate with the same people in the future—in fact, it will make them want to work with you again.

One of the biggest learning areas for us has been disciplining our ego, setting it aside in contentious situations, so that it doesn't prevent us from getting what we want. The ego is power hungry and always wants to win. But, what stops it from "snatching defeat from the jaws of victory?" When ego dominates, we may not recognize victory when it's staring us in the face. Victory also resides in preserving a relationship that may come to fruition another day. That's why we concentrate on growing the pie in any contentious negotiation.

Putting It into Practice

1. Prepare for negotiation. Experts say that those who prepare for their negotiations tend to have better outcomes. This means knowing before you enter the conversation that you have your target fee in mind, as well as the lowest fee you're comfortable accepting. In many cases (for instance, when you teach private lessons), the rate you quote may be non-negotiable. Take the time to create these price points for the various services you provide and make sure you are comfortable with what you plan to charge. Will your proposed fees motivate you to bring your A game to the table?

2. Get creative in advance. When thinking about your fees, do some prep work in case you need to get into pie-expansion mode. What additional services could you offer that might enable a prospective employer to expand the budget? What alternative forms of compensation might they offer you, such as covering your travel or ensuring that you have a high quality video of the production?

3. Be ready with your questions. If a struggle arises in the process of reaching a mutually satisfying agreement, be prepared to ask

your negotiating partner about his or her priorities. He or she ought to know that you are sensitive to priorities on the other side of the deal. Have your questions ready so you can lead this conversation from a place of curiosity even if emotions run high.

To access our Negotiations Cheat Sheet, and other free extras, be sure to check out
http://www.icadenza.com/ebook-resources/

Chapter 8
Pillar #5: Be Accountable for Your Actions

Putting It into Action

By now, your business brain should be starting to awaken. Perhaps your mindset has shifted and you see that becoming more goal-oriented about your career requires a change on the inside.

But change requires more than a focus on what's going on inside our minds. Our thoughts, ideas, and intentions need to be translated into action. And not just any action—busy work is not what this is about. If we take strategic action, on a daily basis, when the big opportunities present themselves, we will be ready for them. Even baby steps, when taken strategically, will gradually set us up for opportunity.

What Is Your Goal?

Once you have formulated your big vision, you can translate it into specific, actionable tasks; in other words, short-term goals. As we discussed in chapter 4, we encourage you to have a stretch vision—something that is fifty percent believable and fifty percent in the realm of the unbelievable.

Divide your vision into small components, with each requiring specific tasks. Map out your vision, and then, with laser-like focus, set priorities, and establish a game plan that will take you where you want to go.

Have you heard of SMART goals? SMART stands for "specific, measurable, achievable, realistic, and timely." A SMART goal could be meeting a deadline such as, "By December I intend to have ten students in my studio who are paying eighty dollars per hour for lessons." Or, "My goal is to book four concerts for myself by February."

You might feel overwhelmed to own a really big goal, even if you've made it SMART. Therefore, we suggest a process to make a big goal manageable.

First, ask yourself whether you are setting yourself up for success: does the timeline make sense? Will you be able to devote the time and energy to do the work to make it happen?

Next, consider your goal in the context of your other desires, commitments, and obligations. Will you be able to make this goal a priority? Can you lay the foundations for success by aligning the other areas of your life in support of your goal? Which areas of your life conflict with your goal?

Conflicting priorities and intentions can impede progress, or worse: they can stop you in your tracks or keep you running in place. Try to resolve the contradictions that might result in frustration and disappointment.

Discipline

Years of musical training have taught us that an artistic career is not all about free-form creativity. We don't get a pass on technique and discipline because we are creative. In fact, intense focus, repetition, and structure are crucial for developing our craft. This same principle also applies to professional growth.

The most successful artists, especially those in popular music, who oversee not just music careers but dozens of other initiatives, whether artistic, business, or charity, have their hands in everything that has their name on it. Yes, they have teams of people helping, but a successful artist is one who steers the ship and drives strategy. The most successful stars are disciplined, driven, prepared, and involved in all facets of their careers—so you should be, too.

Setting Priorities

To tackle a big goal, you must create a manageable strategy. Musicians can feel overwhelmed after they claim their dream project, and then realize that they have no idea how to achieve it.

The good news is that big things happen after the completion of a long list of tiny tasks. Drafting emails to send to people, scheduling meetings, making phone calls to ask for help, doing bits of research here and there, assembling a website, booking the hall—such are the many steps that must be taken to build up to the moment when you can ascend the stage and do what you love to do.

Many of these tasks are administrative in nature, and, therefore, easy prey to procrastination. But, they are no less important than your artistic responsibilities. Without them, there is little or no progress from point A to point B. Someone must attend to these details, and that someone, for now, is you.

The Tyranny of the To-Do List

Inevitably, a big project has a multitude of tiny pieces that comprise it. Writing them all down is a good idea, but, it can lead to one very long to-do list. From personal experience, we know that a to-do list of thirty or more items is completely discouraging. Where do we begin? When we live by the to-do list, we may begin one task, but, then another will catch our eye. An hour later, we will not have completed either.

While a to-do list is good for organization, and is helpful for keeping track of all the things that need to be done, it is terrible for productivity. Instead, we propose something different.

The One Thing

A few years ago, Greg Kastelman, our Director of Concert Booking at Cadenza Artists, discovered a book that completely changed how he approaches his day. The book is *The One Thing*, by Gary Keller and Jay Papasan. The entire book is worth reading, but the main recommendation is this: at the start of each day, ask, "What is the *one* thing that I can do today that will meaningfully move my project forward?" Once you've identified that one thing, do it! Your job is to do that one thing without worrying about anything else on the list.

The book does not suggest that you only need to do one thing a day, or that the one thing will take up your entire day. It speaks to clarity of focus. If you do that one thing and dedicate all of your mental energy to its successful completion, you will perform that task better and faster. Then, you can move on to the next thing. We often fail to realize how much time and effectiveness we lose by switching back and forth between tasks without completing them. We lose focus and disperse our mental energy—we spread ourselves too thin. It is impossible to have laser-like focus on more than one task at a time. So, keep your focus sharp and stay on task—as much as possible—until completion. Then, move on.

This concept demands that you identify the single most important task to complete each day. If you attend to that task first, when your mind is fresh, and your enthusiasm is high, then your focus, willpower, and capacity to do your best thinking are at their peak. Plus, if you are able to complete the task, or a substantial portion of it, then you receive the added bonus of beginning each day with a win!

What if every year, you accomplish 365 really important things (and many other little things later in each day)? That amounts to a lot of targeted action.

What Is Accountability?

As you develop the practice of identifying and committing to that one thing, you may want to consider how some added accountability can keep you on course. Accountability is a system you create for yourself to help you stay on task.

Inevitably, we all have those moments when we want to quit, we're feeling stuck, and we are questioning why we signed on to this crazy idea in the first place. Often, a new, shiny idea or distraction is grabbing our attention. An accountability system is what holds us in place and keeps us going.

Accountability brings up a bigger question, one that is philosophical as well as practical: what do you need to do and who do you need to be to reach your goal? Accountability is not only about the various action steps you need to be taking consistently, but it is also about how you are showing up in your life and career. Does your word hold integrity, not just with others but with yourself? If you make a promise to do something, do you do it? If you don't do it, do you own it and make up for it, or do you just let it slide?

While integrity matters in your relationship with others, it is even more important in how you relate to yourself. Do you trust yourself? Can you count on yourself to stick to a plan that you lay out? Or do you set goals expecting to flake out on yourself?

Of course, we are allowed to change our minds and not do something we promised ourselves we would do. After all, it doesn't hurt anyone else, right? But, it does hurt us. We wear down our trust in ourselves and our ability to act upon our goals. If we can't trust that we will send that email tomorrow, can we trust ourselves to achieve the big goal?

Accountability in Practice

One of our clients, Tom Hooten, is principal trumpet of the Los Angeles Philharmonic. In addition to being a superbly talented musician, Tom views musical ability as the reflection of who you are, not just your talent or how hard you work.

In his own educational experience, in which he had to rebuild his technique from the ground up after developing some bad habits, he came to realize the importance of honesty and integrity with himself for the sake of his musicianship. Tom talks about honesty with regards to self-awareness. Are we honest with ourselves about our strengths and weaknesses? Do we act in integrity with our goals, both musical and professional?

Moving forward, either artistically or professionally, requires complete honesty with where we are today, and a commitment to maintain integrity with what we say we want. To learn more about Tom's work with musicians on honesty and integrity, visit www.tomhooten.com.

Accountability Strategies

Accountability is a vehicle to get on track in order to build up a reservoir of trust in our own words and actions. It provides a means of developing discipline and reliability—crucial qualities that will make us successful and will make others want to work with us.

One way to practice greater accountability with ourselves is to set the bar really low for our daily tasks. We've worked with musicians whose lives are so busy with various jobs and commitments that they barely have time to practice, which becomes a major source of guilt and frustration.

They will say to us, "From now on, I commit to practicing two hours every day! I can do it! I have to!" Realistically though, going from months of erratic practice to two hours a day is a massive lifestyle change. For most of us, committing to such a drastic change in our schedule amounts to setting ourselves up to fail. Instead, we propose a commitment of practicing ten minutes a day. We say, "You can always practice for longer, but you only need to practice for ten minutes to check that off from your list." While they usually roll their eyes at the suggestion of something so minimal, they realize how much easier it is for them to successfully practice ten minutes a day, every day, than two hours a day.

The difference matters from a psychological perspective; can we train ourselves to experience "winning" on a daily basis and build the self-confidence that comes along with having a plan and sticking to it? We experience a unique feeling of gratification and satisfaction when we cross something off our to-do list.

This may sound strange to a high-achieving musician, but setting the bar low on daily action toward your goal is a useful way to learn to keep your word to yourself. Plus, as we've discussed, any project, no matter how huge, can always be broken down into baby steps.

Another way you can use accountability is to find someone who can support you. It's best if you can identify someone who is not invested in your life (significant others, parents, close friends, and

collaborators might not be the best for the task).
You want someone who can be there to support
you and your goal above all else, without being
emotionally attached to your success or failure.

Many of our clients sign on to work with us
largely for this reason. In addition to seeking
guidance from us, they are looking for a partner
who will hold them accountable to the pursuit of
their goals. Having to get on the phone with us
every two weeks motivates them to get things
together so that they have something to show for
their time between sessions.

An accountability partnership is a reporting
mechanism. You must look your partner in the eye
and say whether you got that thing done or not.
While it is easy to break promises to ourselves, it
is more difficult to let another person down.

If you'd like to find an accountability partner,
we suggest feeling out people in a community to
which you belong. Often, it is better to work with
someone you don't know well. Or, feel free to
contact us and we can try to find a match for you
within our network of musicians. Over the years,
we've been matchmakers for several successful
accountability partnerships, and we love to help
people find that valuable support.

Putting It into Practice

1. Develop a ritual each morning of connecting
   with your vision and goal, focusing on the
   specific and timely elements of the goal (i.e.,
   get clear on how quickly the goal is to come
   together. The more specific you can be, the
   better).

2. Then ask yourself, "If I were to only do one thing today, what is *the* most important thing I can do? What is the one thing that will move my project forward most significantly?"

3. Consider identifying an accountability partner with whom you can check in every week or two weeks (in person, by email, or by phone) to keep them apprised of your progress. Evaluate how that commitment compels you to stick to your goals.

To access our Accountability Questions Work Sheet, and other free extras, be sure to check out **http://www.icadenza.com/ebook-resources/**

Chapter 9
Pillar #6: Be Open to Learning

Beginner Status Is OK

According to Malcolm Gladwell's definition, it takes ten thousand hours of doing something to achieve mastery. Therefore, if you're a professional or an aspiring professional musician, it's fair to say that you have either achieved mastery or are close to achieving mastery of your instrument.

Music is a field built on a model of apprenticeship as a way to reach expertise over the course of several years. While we all started as beginners, we can only claim to be professionals once we've travelled a very long road and learned the ins and outs of our craft. While there are countless milestones on the long road to mastery, we don't want to put ourselves out there until we can genuinely call ourselves professionals.

Gaining proficiency in business, especially as an entrepreneur, is an entirely different matter. It is a world of trial and error, of mistakes, and course corrections. And, it requires a variety and multitude of skills, at least some of which you probably don't have (yet!).

The good news is that to succeed in business, you need no specialized knowledge. Succeeding in business, however, does require:

- the willingness to learn
- the willingness to experiment, fail, and try again
- the willingness to lean on others who have the knowledge and skills you seek
- the determination and gumption to keep plugging along until you see results
- In short, it requires a beginner's mindset.

Openness to Growth and Learning

Since we created our two businesses, we've worked with numerous artists in a variety of capacities— as consultants; as teachers of workshops, seminars, and online courses; and as cheerleaders. We also continue to represent over fifty artists as their agents and managers. We've spent a lot of time thinking about what differentiates the most successful artists from the ones who are struggling.

Each of the chapters in this book focuses on a different quality that, we find, sets a musician up for success. And without a doubt, one of the most important qualities is a desire for personal growth and the willingness to learn the essentials in order to achieve it.

Personal Growth

Personal growth requires self-awareness. Self-awareness means courageously and dispassionately analyzing your behaviors, habits, attitudes, beliefs, and mindset, as well as the impressions you make on others, from your interpersonal approach to your artistry—in short, everything about you that propels you forward or holds you back in your career. Personal growth also requires the willingness to make the necessary and realistic adjustments that will free you from the mental and emotional restrictions that hinder your forward motion.

Are you open to feedback from trusted advisors and coaches on your areas of strength and opportunities for improvement? Are you open to seeing your weaknesses as opportunities for change and personal growth? If so, you'll have reason to rejoice when you find them because converting them into strengths will create the forward motion you desire.

Are you aware of the impression you make on others? Do you know which of your individual characteristics make you successful and which may be holding you back? Personal growth requires deep self-awareness—as well as self-acceptance--to find areas for improvement.

As agents and managers, we are on the front lines, advocating for our artists' talent. But we are often required to convey unpleasant feedback from presenters—even to very established artists. When the roadblock is the result of the artist's behavior—as communicated to us by those in a position to advance his or her career—it is our duty to pass the message to the one person who will benefit the most from hearing it: the artist.

We are always supportive of our artist, but honest as well, because we are all on the same team, and share the same goal: the artist's success. No one likes negative feedback. But, how do we give negative feedback to someone who refuses to hear it? In that case, our job is more difficult, and sometimes impossible. If an artist is unwilling to utilize the feedback he or she receives, let alone even to hear it, our advocacy for that artist will necessarily be insufficient to propel his or her career forward. To do our job, we need the artist to see criticism as an opportunity for personal growth, and, therefore, an opportunity for greater success.

Acquiring New Skills

In addition to personal growth, building your career with the assistance of your business brain will also require the development of a host of other skills and competencies.

The good news is that these skills, as onerous as they may seem right now, are easy compared to the difficulty required to perform your craft. These skills are also relatively easy to master; there are plentiful resources out there to help you acquire them speedily.

So what additional skills might you need? It really depends on you and your goals, but these could include:

- managing your finances
- building a website
- photography and photo editing
- basic graphic design for posters, flyers, and other promotional materials
- writing skills
- public speaking
- video editing
- social media promotion
- putting together a promotional package
- supervising an assistant effectively

The internet is an amazing resource. It is easy to find instructional information for all of these skills and more. You can also search out books and courses (either online, or at a local university extension program) to fill in these areas.

Also think about how you can benefit from the wisdom of other people to expand your knowledge base. Do you have a friend who can talk to you about photography, accounting, or social media? Don't be afraid to ask for help and guidance, but also, don't pass on the pleasure of trying out a new skill as a beginner.

What Standard of Competency Are You Seeking?

Musicians harbor high artistic standards, and rightly so. But should they uphold those same standards for all of their other activities? If so, it may be logical for the artist to conclude: "If I can't do it perfectly, it's not worth doing at all." True or false?

Your artistry requires a level of perfection that does not necessarily apply to other aspects of your career. Furthermore, many areas allow for inexperience and can accommodate improvement over time. For example, an artist can benefit from having a website. Building it is another matter. You may not know how to build it, but you can learn. And it does not have to be the most perfect, best possible website of all time. The internet provides instructions so that, in a matter of hours, you can design your own professional-looking website, at little cost. You can improve on it over time as your proficiency for content and design improves.

But, there is no reason for not developing a website on your own once you discard the notion that it must be the perfect website. Imagine the accomplishment of progressing from having no meaningful web presence whatsoever to one that is accurate and professional and that can make it easier for people to hire you. This is but one element that can contribute to the growth of your career and it is something you can do now. Eventually, you will have the means to hire a professional to create the website that meets your standards of perfection. For now, create it on your own and think of it as a work in progress.

The Rabbit Hole of Unproductive Work

You don't need to be an expert in every aspect of your business. You only need to be proficient enough to get the job done so that you aren't delayed waiting for someone else to do what you can do for yourself. Your rudimentary proficiency will eventually enable you to communicate effectively with those who have expertise in those areas so that you can learn from them, and, ultimately, hire them when you are in the financial position to do so.

As you develop new skills, try to avoid endless hours of work that do not advance your career. Do not be tempted to delve too deeply into the types of skills listed above, because they are time-eaters. Do what is required, but concentrate on your art and your serious goals. You must learn to spend your precious time in the most effective manner.

Remember, your objective should be the proficiency level needed to do the task at hand. Your job is not to become an expert in that new skill, unless you deliberately choose to be—and then, you run the risk of diverting time and effort away from your musical career.

Though it may sound like something a slacker would say, we urge you to distinguish the areas of your career that truly require expertise from those that allow you to be "good enough." Appreciate that your time is limited and will become more so as your artistic opportunities grow.

Before starting iCadenza, we had no experience with web development, aside from the one JavaScript class Julia took in college. When we built our first website, we were so thrilled to get the hang of it that we pulled several all-nighters to make it perfect. A few months later, we changed it completely. We learned a valuable lesson: perfecting all the tiny details—thus creating more and more that need to be perfected—is not always worth the effort.

The Larger Benefit

Although acquiring new skills can help you move your business forward, there is another benefit: it empowers your beginner's mindset, which encourages risk-taking and propels you out of your comfort zone. The act of learning is a proficiency in itself that expands as you venture into unfamiliar territory.

The first time we created a table on our website with HTML, we jumped for joy. We were so proud of having figured out how to do it on our own. Sure, it wasn't really that complicated, but it was empowering nonetheless. That moment enabled us to shift from thinking of ourselves as "non-technically savvy" to "the kind of people who can figure most things out." That moment gave us confidence that we could break through other perceived limitations.

We also adopted the mindset that it is fun to go outside our comfort zone by learning new skills. Now, we say, "I can learn anything," and, "Even though I haven't done this before, I can figure it out." We have learned to enjoy the process and see it as fun.

Through the gradual process of learning new skills, we build our risk tolerance as we practice handling curveballs with confidence. In unfamiliar situations for which we are unprepared, we find ourselves stepping up to the plate with the certainty that we can figure it out.

We support and encourage clients to build new skills that once seemed beyond their abilities. Musicians ask us to assist them in organizing tours for their ensembles. We support them every step of the way. Not only do we research presenters, but we help our clients practice their sales pitch with mock phone calls and role-play. We help them draft emails, and guide them through the process of fee negotiations, and a multitude of other situations—many unanticipated.

While our process offers a lot of handholding, our clients eventually realize that they are more than capable of doing all of the above on their own. Engaging in these processes breeds success, and their successes inspire them to engage even more. Our clients succeed because they learn to do the work for themselves.

Afraid to Say "Yes"?

It is easy to view a learning opportunity with fear. After all, we are dealing with the unknown. Our client Jim realized that his fear of a learning opportunity was holding him back:

I was given a gift certificate for a free consultation with iCadenza through a friend. Believe it or not, I held onto it for a year and a half. I didn't realize that fear was debilitating me from making a conscious choice to move ahead. I knew it would cost money and I was thinking, "Where am I going to come up with this money?" My attitude was this was too difficult, too expensive, it's this, it's that. As I worked with Julia and Jennifer, I began to realize I was worth so much more than I'd been giving myself credit for. They made me realize I was worth making this investment in myself. And as I came to find, they were well worth the price. [When it came to coming up with the money, I learned that] I had so many people who believed in me, that I actually had people who paid for all six months. People literally said, I want to give you this as a gift. I want to pay for two months. I realized I need to give myself a little more credit.

Putting It into Practice

Spend five to ten minutes journaling on the following questions:

1. Where are my opportunities for personal growth? What habits and behaviors can I build that will make me more productive, more effective in my work, and more fulfilled in my life? How might I develop these areas?

2. What skills do I need to shepherd my professional life in the direction in which I want it to go? How much time should I spend learning these skills?

3. What is the most efficient and effective way to gain the knowledge I seek?

Chapter 10
Facing Fear

Now that we've discussed the six pillars to success as a business-minded artist, we must turn to the "dark side" and address those gloomy days when the gray clouds obscure the blue skies.

By now, you know that we believe in optimism and positivity, and that we work hard to stay positive. But let's be real. Hard times come, and sometimes we feel discouraged. There are days when we wonder whether it's all worth it, whether we're really cut out for the artistic life, and whether there's any way out of a difficult situation.

What do you do when you fall off track? Where do you find the energy and enthusiasm to get up again? What if we feel too overwhelmed to get back on the horse?

What is the resistance that prevents us from overcoming the darkness and returning to the light of optimism? We learned about resistance from a fantastic book, *The War of Art*, by novelist Steven Pressfield. In it, he defines resistance as that which attempts to stop us as we pursue our creative fulfillment.

Resistance can arise from within ourselves, in the form of self-doubt, or the avoidance of an essential task that we know needs to be accomplished. It can come from our immediate environment and the people around us. Those near and dear may be critical of our dreams. Resistance can also come from the intrusion of other responsibilities that leave us little time to pursue our goals.

Let's break these down.

Experiencing Internal Resistance

Internal resistance may be rooted in fear. It can be fear of failure or fear of success or something entirely different. It could be fear of the unknown. Uncertainty easily inspires fear. (See chapter 4 to help you gain clarity and connect to your inner passion. That sense of passion can help reconnect you to the reasons you have for striving to overcome your fear.)

No matter the source of your fear, Pressfield would ask you to consider how a professional would handle the situation versus an amateur.

One of our clients, soprano Karen Hogle Brown, shares the following about her attempts to integrate Pressfield's philosophy into her own process when dealing with self-doubt and self-sabotage:

It is so easy for me to go to dark places on a bad singing day. Echoes of, "I'm just not good enough," or, "No matter what I do, I'll never succeed in this," run amuck through my brain, sometimes on a daily basis. Pressfield describes this thinking as "amateur." He further described that a "professional" would ask themselves questions such as, "What can I learn from what happened today?" and, "How am I going to go about addressing this problem?"

Just the other day, I was having difficulty in my practice. I was unsure of many things, from whether my diction was clear enough, to if my sound was focused enough. My normal reaction in my head is to say, "You call yourself a singer? You should know exactly how to place this passage by now! You've only been practicing for twenty years." I let those thoughts linger for just a moment, and then picked up the phone and made an appointment for a [vocal] coaching. I realized that I'm probably being hypersensitive, and having an outside ear will be able to rationally tell me whether or not I need to change something, or if things are fine.

I have found this change of thought process to be my biggest change in behavior since completing the iCadenza eCourse and reading Pressfield's book. As hard as I worked, and as much as I thought of myself as a "professional," I was guilty of some rather "amateur" behavior.

Now I really try to address problems and frustrations by changing my inner monologue to include questions. "What do I need to make this work? What is standing in my way? What is the next step to achieving this goal? Instead of wasting precious time and energy on self-pity, why not turn the outlook around to moving forward?"

I won't say it has been easy, but I figure changing a thought pattern is one of the hardest habits to break. Together with awareness of the barriers, and practicing a more positive response to them, I am hoping that I can maintain a positive outlook and prevent some self-sabotage.

A common response to internal resistance is avoidance. (Karen hints at this in her story.) This usually leads to stagnation and the feeling of being "stuck." You resign yourself to a feeling of helplessness, believing that you are a victim of your thoughts and feelings. It's a losing attitude that makes you feel bad about yourself, bad about your career, and bad about your future.

An alternative is to become curious about your own process. Like a detective, you can doggedly strive to get to the bottom of what's stopping you from taking the action you need. As Karen did, ask yourself some questions:

- What's in my way?
- What do I need to do to make this work?
- What are the next steps towards my dream?
- Is the story that I believe about myself, and the obstacle in my way, true? Are there parts of it that might be false or a misrepresentation of the truth?
- Why is this _____ stopping me? (Fill in the blank with the fear, concern, or self-talk message.)
- If fear is palpable, can you listen to its message? In every fear there tends to be a very specific question, concern, or warning. We may get sucked into the physical experience of fear so quickly that we forget to actually ask, "What am I afraid of?" and, "Why is it stopping me from taking action?" Sometimes that thing you're afraid of is actually a component of your goal. And, as discussed in chapter 7, you may be able to negotiate with that part of you that's afraid

in order to find a solution that relieves the block, allowing you to get back into action.

Experiencing External Resistance

Resistance may come from our surrounding environment--either circumstances or the people around us. Beware that external resistance can masquerade as a "sign" that you're on the wrong track, which can seduce you into self-doubt. Here are some examples:

- You (or a loved one) is ill
- Your house needs an urgent repair
- The kids need to be picked up early
- Anything "outside" that's disrupting your goals

A common story we've heard (and sometimes reenacted ourselves, as we face our own external resistance) is something like: "I want to audition for my dream part but my car broke down and I have to work late three nights this week. Is this a sign that I should bag the whole audition? Maybe it's not meant to be!"

A few years ago, we worked with a client named Ashley. A fabulous pianist, she had started to gain a reputation for being an extraordinary educator for kids ranging from elementary through high school age. She had a knack for tapping into each child's motivations, strengths, and weaknesses, and she created amazing, totally customized programs for them. She took ordinary kids and helped them develop to the point where they were winning major competitions in their age groups. She brought amazing value to her work, and so much passion, but she was getting pummeled by resistance.

She wanted to teach more advanced students for the higher fees which she needed. She created action plans to reach out to some of the more prestigious educational institutions, but circumstances always intervened.

She had a bothersome neighbor who wasted her time. Family drama would regularly break out. When nothing else was in the way, she would tell herself a compelling story: interviews and meetings, as well as her own piano practice, would cause her to neglect her young daughter. Her car even broke down!

All of these things were true. But she didn't perceive them as minor occurrences with simple and direct solutions. Instead, they took up space in her mind and heart as major obstacles. Self-doubt took hold. She began to doubt that she had selected the right vocation, and viewed external circumstances as a sign that she was taking steps too bold for her life.

We supported her in unraveling her resistance patterns. She was then able to free herself for action. Afterwards, it only took her a few months to get that coveted position she'd wanted. She even started to plan a solo recital for herself that she had wanted to perform for a long time.

Therefore, when it comes to dealing with external resistance, we encourage you to ask yourself:

- Are the stories I'm telling myself accurate? Is this really the way the world works or is this merely my perception of the way the world works?
- How can I react differently?
- What can I gain from this challenge?

Resistance from Loved Ones

Steven Pressfield offers a vivid metaphor to describe the source of external resistance when it comes from the people around you. He describes a bucket filled with crabs. When one crab attempts to climb out of the bucket, the other crabs go berserk trying to keep it down inside the bucket. The crabs aren't malicious in their desire to keep the runaway crab in the bucket. They're simply reacting to the threat of change. They want the crab to "come back" so that their environment remains as it was. Pressfield likens the wayward crab to the artist. He believes that when you stand in your value and display a commitment to your dreams, other people often feel uncomfortable.

Many of us live at the whim and will of others; when people see someone--in a perceived act of rebellion--take ownership of his or her potential, the ecosystem is disrupted and equilibrium must be restored. We are biologically programmed to seek equilibrium—our physiological survival rests on homeostasis. Change is not just hard mentally, it's going against the grain of our natural instincts, and is uncomfortable for those around us because their instincts perceive a threat to their environment.

Steven Pressfield asks, "What does this mean for you?" If you feel that the metaphor applies, you simply need to be aware that some of the resistance you find reflects other people's discomfort. If so, recognize that it's not a sign that you're on the wrong path. To the extent that you can, cultivate patience with yourself and with the people in your life.

Identify How You Respond to Resistance

How do you typically respond to resistance?

Imagine that you have encountered a brick wall protected by a fire-breathing dragon. There are five ways that people tend to respond when faced with a challenge:

- **Bulldozing:** get through the wall with sheer force
- **Denying:** pretend it's not there and linger just out of sight ("Wall? What wall?")
- **Blaming others:** *You* put this wall here, didn't you? This must be *your* dragon!
- **Seeing omens:** you believe that if there is a wall, it's a sign that this is the wrong path
- **Lamenting:** cry and think that you're the only one who's ever had to deal with this wall

Tip: You might notice that you employ a combination of tactics (most of us do).

You will always be confronted by obstacles at various stages in your life and career. It goes with being alive. The question is, how committed are you to your dream? How willing are you to move through the challenges? Try to see challenges as tests. Imagine how different life would be if you could move through them with grace and feel empowered when you reach the other side.

Having, ourselves, resorted to bulldozing, denying, blaming, seeing omens, and lamenting when faced with brick walls, we can only encourage you to try the strategies that we employ: take small action steps and move at a slow, comfortable pace to get through the wall. Be gentle with yourself as you bring awareness to your reaction to resistance. Acknowledge that discomfort is a sure sign of growth. Check back with your affirmations, which you may need now more than ever.

And, most importantly, consider what you gain by surmounting this obstacle—in addition to your goal on the other end:

- Courage
- Wisdom
- New skills
- Faith
- Patience
- Sensitivity

How you view your situation is crucial. Your mind is your greatest ally or your cruelest adversary. But by no means should you punish yourself when you're having a tough time with your thoughts. Instead, use your curiosity to discover a deeper understanding of yourself, and look for insights.

Put It into Practice

Spend five to ten minutes writing in your journal on each of these questions.

1. How does resistance appear to you? List the different forms it takes.
2. What might you gain by crossing through to the other side of a seemingly insurmountable obstacle?
3. Practice writing ten endings for the following phrase: If I knew I couldn't fail, I would...

Chapter 11
Receiving and Celebrating Success

"Success consists of going from failure to failure without loss of enthusiasm." – Winston Churchill

Asking and Receiving

Now that we've explored the dark side, let's talk about what happens when things go well!

There are two principles that we dismissed out of hand when we first learned about them. To our shock and embarrassment, once we gave them a fair shot, they were extremely effective. We still struggle with them, occasionally, but we knew that we had to share them with you.

Principle #1: Learning How to Ask

A lot of people struggle with the idea of asking for things. Asking for something can feel like weakness. When we admit that we need help, we feel vulnerable. Moreover, we musicians often think of ourselves as lone warriors for whom the mark of success is in knowing that we achieved it all on our own. The other side of that coin is that if we didn't achieve our success on our own, then we don't deserve to call it ours, and we don't deserve to be praised for it.

We are also attached to the idea that we only deserve success if we worked really, really hard to get it. Blood, sweat, and tears are required. If someone helped us on the way, it's almost as though we cheated!

So the question is: are you limiting your success by holding fast to the idea of doing something great alone? Or are you open to doing something great by allowing others to help you?

Let Others In

When you ask for help, you're letting someone else participate in your big project. It is exciting to let others in—exciting for you as well as them. It makes them want to root for you.

But we can hear your resistance setting in. "It is hard to ask for help. And it can be scary. Asking for help means imposing on another person unfairly and setting yourself up for possible rejection because, after all, the answer could be 'no.'"

The risk is valid, but the truth is that you really have very little to lose. If your request for help is not granted, you're right back where you started. Nothing gained, but also nothing lost.

When we started our business, we were already used to success. We were used to success in high school and college; we were used to getting things right the first time, and—we'll admit it—we were used to being liked. But, in our new endeavor, we were afraid. We were afraid of many things, including failure. Nevertheless, we had made the commitment to strike out. Still, we only wanted to ask for things if the answer was going to be "yes." In fact, we were terrified of rejection.

When our business coaches suggested the idea of asking for help as a principle to live by, we responded with questions. We said we were willing to try, but wanted to know how to guarantee an affirmative response. We also wanted a formula for selecting the right person of whom to make the request in order to avoid risking a negative response. In other words, we were looking for a proven method to make a risk-free request. Of course, no such thing exists.

Our coaches annoyed us with a challenge. They asked us to see how many "no" responses we could score. They argued that even if the odds were against us, we would, nonetheless, receive some "yes" responses despite the chorus of "no." In other words, if we did not risk receiving a "no", we would not receive any "yes" responses at all.

For example, to achieve a one percent success rate, we would have to approach one hundred people to get to that one response in the affirmative. We didn't relish the idea but we decided to try it.

At the time, we were doing video interviews with artists. To appease our coaches, we started asking major stars to do video interviews with us. We expected that our quest for "noes" would be unhappily successful. We assumed that we'd get a lot of rejections and would quickly report back to our coaches that, yes, we can fail repeatedly on command.

The result of our activity was the opposite of what we had expected. It was amazingly hard to get a "no!" Defeated in the challenge, we arrived at our next session having failed at the task—we had very few "noes" to show for our risk-taking and a lot of "yeses." Case in point.

If You Ask, You Shall Receive

I (Jennifer) admire Julia's willingness to make big asks—some which never would have occurred to me. I want to share one incident that opened my eyes to the power of asking.

We were in St. Louis for a conference and Tim O'Leary, executive director of Opera St. Louis, was giving a keynote address. Delayed by a meeting, we managed to sneak in to hear the last ten minutes of his talk, in which he offered brilliant and insightful comments. His talk finished around 11:30am.

As people mobbed him, wanting to ask questions and share input, we hung back, preferring to say hello after the crowd had subsided. Feeling my stomach growl, I asked Julia what she wanted to do for lunch. She became excited.

"Oh! We should ask him to lunch!"

My gut reaction was to disagree and rationalize why it was not a good idea to ask him to lunch. We didn't know him at all; we'd be overstepping; he was probably busy. Though my mind was signaling, "Red alert!" I managed to force out a quick, "Sure, why not?" in response.

When he finally emerged from the crowd, we approached and thanked him for his thoughtful presentation, and praised the innovative community building he'd achieved in St. Louis. Then, Julia popped the question:

"We wouldn't want to impose, but could we possibly take you to lunch?"

He looked stunned for a moment. Then he responded, slightly caught off guard.

"Well...I think so. I just need to check with my wife, please give me a moment."

As a result of Julia's willingness to ask, we had the opportunity to have a lovely lunch with the director of an opera company. We learned more about his work and goals, and we talked about our work. In short, we had a friendly and memorable time getting to know an interesting leader in our field.

From that moment on, I've constantly thought: what opportunities am I forfeiting because I do not think to ask? The truth is, people don't really like to say no. Practicing your ask can lead to unexpectedly good results.

Principle #2: Learning How to Receive

Equally important is knowing how to receive, willingly and graciously. How open are you to receiving the generosity of others as it flows to you?

Some of us need to learn how to receive because receiving can feel like taking, if we are not secure in our self-worth. It can feel like we don't deserve to receive the praise or benefit that has come our way.

If you are praised for your performance in a concert, can you reply with a sincere and simple thank you? Or, do you dodge the compliment? Perhaps you tend to diminish yourself with, "Oh, I was off my game tonight," or, "There's so much I could have done better," or, "No, thank *you*! It's all because of you that I could perform so you deserve the real credit!" Or, perhaps you might say a kind "thank you" but in your head be thinking, "That woman knows nothing about music so her praise doesn't really count."

Oprah Winfrey once talked about a realization she had about the importance of accepting thanks and gratitude from others. While she, too, had been in the habit of deflecting the thanks she received from others, she realized that she actually did them a disservice by not fully accepting their praise.

When people approached Oprah to thank her profusely for her program and told her how it had changed their lives, she would respond with a very warm, "No, thank you!" Ultimately, she realized that instead of acknowledging the sincere feelings of her followers, she was invalidating the depth of their experience. She was also denying that she had made that experience possible for them. When she deflected their praise, she was, in effect, rejecting them, and saying that their profound experience was really very small and insignificant. ("Oh, that old thing? It was nothing!")

Remember that when someone thanks or praises you, it is not just about you—it is about them and their experience. To fully honor their experience, you must accept their praise.

Receiving can also challenge your internal experience. When you push yourself to reach milestone after milestone, your successes may tend to be less meaningful. While it's great to continually strive for the next challenge, don't forget to acknowledge yourself for the progress you've worked so hard to achieve. Can you learn to reflect on how far you've come and what you've made happen?

As you put your "business brain" to work, we have no doubt that you will see results in your life and career—even if they start out on a small scale. Please don't miss the opportunities to savor them and appreciate that what you desire is flowing your way.

We encourage you to receive graciously, with gratitude to whom or whatever sent it to you, and to yourself for doing the work to make it happen. It is crucial to admire the fruits of your hard work.

The Penguins Arrive

As we mentioned in chapter 6, we represent *March of the Penguins* in live presentations with symphony orchestras. What we didn't mention before is that this project was several years in the making.

We began to represent the conductor of the original score from the film, Jeffrey Schindler, in 2011 and, soon after, identified the goal of producing *March of the Penguins* with orchestra. It turned out to be a very long ride. Months turned into years as we sought out the rights-holders, negotiated the license with the movie studio, assembled the right technical team to execute it in the concert hall, and negotiated with the symphony. Additionally, Jeffrey had to produce and realize the score. It was a long journey. We felt as though we had walked over seventy miles back and forth, just like the penguins in the film. Finally, on July 8, 2015, we saw the results of our efforts at the project's debut with the Seattle Symphony.

After the show, we spent time with Jeffrey Schindler and his lovely wife Bonnie. Together, we basked in the delight of seeing a project through to its successful completion. And, we shared words of gratitude with each other—since we could only have made this happen together.

We made time to celebrate and commemorate our achievement and we honored everyone and everything that went into the project. We encourage you to find those moments to celebrate every win in your own, unique way, no matter how small the achievement. Enjoy the gratification that comes with knowing that you had a goal, you worked towards it, and you made it happen. A project brought to completion means that you created something that previously did not exist in the world, which is no small feat. Savor the moment so you can re-energize yourself to do it all over again!

At the end of their nine-month penguin baby rearing and feeding process, even the penguins celebrate by swimming blissfully for a three-month period, also known in human terms as summer vacation!

Put It into Practice

1. What are some big asks that you've been saving up? Let's think back to a question from the last chapter: if you knew you couldn't fail, what would you ask for?
2. As you reach the end of this book, what are the milestones in your life and career that you can celebrate now?
3. What are the goals that you're currently working toward?
4. Can you build in a celebration for the milestones achieved now, no matter how small?

Conclusion

You've sacrificed in the name of art. Thousands of others have done the same. But it's up to you to take that sacrifice and turn it into an investment in your future. Are you willing to take your enormous talent and thousands of hours in the practice room and develop the new skills that we've discussed to activate your business brain? We all have blind spots; in the pages that you've read, did anything jump out at you as an area for growth? Are you willing to get a little bit uncomfortable to try doing things differently? It won't be easy, but you don't have to go it alone.

We hope you'll stay in touch with us. Join our free mailing list to get freebies and tips every week. Find our page on Facebook (**www.facebook.com/icadenzafans**) or check us out on Twitter (**@icadenza**) to join the conversation. Need an accountability partner? Let us know and we'll make sure that you get matched up.

Need more support? Check out our online courses and consulting offerings at **http://www.iCadenza.com**.

Thanks for hanging on with us through this journey, and we look forward to hearing from you, or perhaps discovering you and your artistry along the way.

In Memory: Michelle Abend Bauman

Shortly after the digital release of this book, we got news that hit us like a ton of bricks. Our dear friend, mentor, role model, and coach, Michelle Bauman, passed away after a two-year battle with cancer. As we prepared for the paperback release, we knew we had to add a short tribute to this amazing woman who had given so much to us, back when it mattered the most.

There are people who come into your life and leave you forever changed. For us, one of those people was Michelle Bauman. Together with Carolyn Freyer-Jones, she pushed us to the limits of what we thought we could do—and then pushed us further to explore the realm beyond what was believable for us.

We met Michelle and Carolyn in 2010, one year into the hamster wheel that was our start-up experience. We were trying to find a business model that both sustained us financially and allowed us to do meaningful work in the arts and bring value to the world. We were truly struggling. By sheer luck we found out about a women's coaching group that Michelle and Carolyn were leading and, on a lark, we agreed to do it together. That four-month experience led to an ongoing coaching relationship with Carolyn and Michelle that lasted four years, on and off. Their mentorship, guidance, and feedback empowered us through many of the most difficult parts of our journey in our earliest days. The learnings, awareness, and support we gained through our work with them contributed profoundly to our personal and professional development.

We both felt a deep emotional connection to Michelle's journey. She shared with us how much and for how long she had bought into the same myths that we were accepting as truths. It was through her example that we were able to stand in our own intrinsic value and start dismantling the farce that we called "reality." We learned to love ourselves for who we are, not what we do. We learned to accept our own shortcomings and work with them rather than against them. We learned how to believe in ourselves, even when it feels like the world is crashing down and we have nothing to show for our effort. We learned how to be with others in times of discomfort and even failure—and how to be vulnerable, accept responsibility, and work together to repair what has been broken or torn.

Most importantly, we learned to hear our own hearts' songs, as well as each other's. We learned to listen to each other with loving and without attachment. We learned to have the tough conversations and to address what's not working without fearing upheaval or trying to protect—or, worse, control—each other's feelings.

We became conscious of our own self destructive and unproductive patterns wherein we sabotaged ourselves. Michelle provided us with the environment, openness, and loving support to make all of this transformation possible, and so much more. By sharing stories of her path, teaching us strategies for awareness and self-direction, and providing a safe space of compassion, love, and light, we were able to overcome deeply ingrained habits and develop new ones that served us much better.

But Michelle did much more than that. She introduced us to Cheri Jamison, an extraordinary member of our Cadenza Artists team, for whom we are grateful every day. She introduced us to Nancy Kline, whose Time to Think methodology and approach to life has changed the way we work with our team and others. Michelle spurred growth for us in countless ways, some of which we are still discovering.

Learning that Michelle passed away from cancer on December 14th, 2015, was heartbreaking for us. Michelle touched hundreds of lives, as she had ours, in the most profound of ways. Because of Michelle, we are forever changed. We mourn her loss but we are the lucky ones. Michelle filled us with so much love and zest for life that we have enough to last us our lifetimes. Our mission? To pass it on to as many people as we can, in living memory and tribute to our extraordinary mentor.

About the Authors

Jennifer Rosenfeld and Julia Torgovitskaya have worked with over 1000 musicians through individual coaching and hundreds more through online programs, workshops, and university programs. The focus of their company, iCadenza, is to provide top-notch career coaching and skill-building education to musicians looking to grow their career opportunities. Rosenfeld and Torgovitskaya are also the co-founders of Cadenza Artists, a talent agency and artist management company representing over 50 music, dance, and multidisciplinary projects in a range of styles and genres. Their experience representing and booking talent gives them a ground-floor perspective on what artists need to do to advance their careers. Having both started out as musicians and having later received graduate degrees in business and law, Rosenfeld and Torgovitskaya are living and applying the lessons they teach on a daily basis, and they share openly about their individual and collective journey on their blog. Visit iCadenza.com for more information and to join the iCadenza mailing list.